INFINITY

WEALTH

Do you want to get rich? Learn from rich people!

CONTENTS

PROLOGUE

This book is about doing everything you can do to increase your odds of reaching what I call Infinity—a financial place in your future where you won't have to work unless you want to. It will help you establish the right mindset and make the best choices available to you. The reality is that sometimes there are events that we cannot control that impact the financial markets. These events include national emergencies, terrorist attacks, wars, and pandemics, just to name a few. When they occur, they can have a dramatic impact on all aspects of our finances, as well as our personal well-being. There is no such thing as risk-free.

COVID-19 is a fresh reminder of exactly how tenuous our claims to risk-free lives can be. Not only did the virus cause massive losses in the markets, reduce the demand for oil, and cause lockdowns throughout the world, but it also left millions of people out of work and in severe financial distress. Perhaps this was you.

The true impact of the virus on our economy will take years to fully understand, but it teaches us an important lesson. Hope for the best, but prepare for the worst. In the investment world, that simply means you need to know how to take care of yourself regardless. You need to take care of yourself in good times as well as bad. To learn how to do this, all you need is a good teacher, an open mind, and a willingness to be a student of history.

History has repeatedly shown us that American investors overreact to major events in the marketplace. Whether it be the AIDS crisis, SARS, MERS, Ebola, Zika, or measles, the markets tend to take a very pessimistic view in the short term but recover in the long term. This goes for other so-called black swan events, going back to the Arab-Israeli War and the oil embargo, the Iranian hostage crisis, the first Gulf War, the 9/11 attacks, and even the most recent recession. The recovery is always ahead of us, even though sometimes the recovery is slow.

You can rest assured that Wall Street's reaction to pandemics and epidemics has historically been to have a very short memory and quickly forget about the negative and get right on with business, generally speaking, within six months. In fact, if you look at six-month snapshots from the diseases I just listed, you'll see that in all but one case, the markets were back in positive territory within six months. The one exception was the AIDS crisis, where it was down less than half a percent over a six-month period.

The question is not whether the markets will recover; it's how long it will take them to recover. And how can you stay sane during that recovery period when you know full well that the cable news talking heads will be preaching doom and gloom simply because it sells better than optimism?

Warren Buffett once wrote to his investors that when other people are fearful, we should be greedy, and when other people are greedy, we should be fearful. That's a fancy way of saying don't trust all the volatility, don't trust all the pessimists, and also don't trust all the optimists. The truth usually lies somewhere in the middle, and disciplined investing wins out over the long haul.

The success I have had has always been the result of taking the long view. And what's the longest view we can take? Infinity! That's why I call my approach Infinity Investing. I tell my students that their holding period is forever. When they buy something, their intent should not be to roll it over at a profit. This doesn't mean you'll never sell an asset. It just means that the purpose of the purchase is not to sell it. They will use the asset to make money in a way that becomes ongoing. As a result, they can avoid reckless decisions that are not based on facts. Even more importantly, if they do sell, they're really not selling an asset—they're trading it for something else because they see a better opportunity elsewhere.

In a perfect world, you'd simply accumulate assets and live off them. You'd pass them on to future generations or to organizations you care about and let them benefit from that same income stream that you lived off of. But I know the world is not perfect, and any plan needs to have the flexibility to accommodate unforeseen events. It's the same thing that an airline pilot has to deal with if their 747 takes off from Seattle for New York and the winds shift to the south. The pilot, still wanting to go to New York, has to make course corrections along the way. We never know what our headwinds are going to be. We never know what the weather might hold and whether there's a squall in our way. Ultimately, we do know we'll make it to our destination as we navigate around those obstacles.

Investing is no different. We need to first identify where we're going to go, then set the right course, and then make course corrections as necessary along the way. The prudent investors among us will do so even during a crisis and its aftermath and will be the ones rewarded over time.

One of the first multimillionaires I met (who was also self-made) told me, "Don't look at the value of your accounts. Don't look at the value of your real estate. Look at what they produce." As long as my assets are producing, I'm not overly concerned. The people who have to worry are the ones who are the speculators and the gamblers who need the asset to move up or down in order to make money. That means they are losing sleep when the market takes dramatic turns in either direction. That is not Infinity Investing.

Some people would tell you they love the volatility of the ups and downs, the adrenaline rush when their holdings increase and the pits in their stomachs when they fall. Those are not investors. Those are professional gamblers who are trying to take advantage of short-term directional changes in the market. And I would say to any investor, you don't want to go head-to-head with professional gamblers. Let them do what they want to do, and we will do what we want to do. And overall we will have great success. It doesn't mean they won't. It just means we should not be competing head-to-head with somebody whose life revolves around making their living on the short-term directional changes of the market.

If you taught yourself some basic basketball skills and you practiced shooting every day in your driveway, you might develop a nice shot. You build up your confidence (in your mind as a basketball player), and you decide you are ready to play with the big boys. You go to the gym and step in the court to play. You declare, "I am ready to play some basketball," and out walks LeBron James, who says, "So am I." Do you think you have a chance of winning? Yet that is what amateur traders do on an almost daily basis. They learn some "trading techniques" and end up going head-to-head with some of the best traders in the world. In that world there are definitely winners and losers, and the overwhelming odds are you will be the loser.

Do not play that game.

Instead, focus on win-win scenarios in the market. Essentially, you let LeBron James do what he does, and you invest in the league. Everybody wins.

Infinity Investing is about making money no matter what the market is doing and for an infinite period of time. As you will discover in this book, Infinity Investing relies heavily on market history to guide us. We use that to minimize risk and to ensure a consistent return year after year, decade after decade, and, God willing, century after century.

INTRODUCTION

I grew up with many mentors, ranging from my coaches, teachers, and friends to my father and parents of my friends. I learned a major lesson from a few major mentors, but they were very different people and taught me that same lesson in very different ways. One such mentor was my father, who worked for the same *Fortune* 100 company from the day he graduated from college until he retired. My dad was proud to have graduated from college, as he was one of the first to do so in his family. He was focused on his kids graduating from college and getting good jobs with big companies.

By contrast, one of my other mentors was the father of a good friend. My friend's father was an independent businessman who never mentioned college (although he must have graduated because, after achieving financial success, he earned an MBA and even attended law school—briefly). He liked to tell anyone who listened that the professors were all full of BS. He owned an auction and liquidation company with a few stores and knew the ins and outs of just about every type of business imaginable. He liquidated and auctioned off inventory and assets for everyone from Nordstrom, Costco, and Home Depot to school districts, local police stations, and even the IRS. Keep in mind that this was before the internet brought us the likes of eBay and Overstock.com, so he moved millions of dollars of product around the world with a phone and fax machine. It was fascinating on many levels, but what stuck out was his disdain for the ways that schools taught business and how they neglected the role of relationships, confidence, and creative thinking. He did not think government was efficient and was involved in politics until he passed, but not in an angry sort of way you see so much of today; rather, he was more interested in making things efficient with the same creativity he brought to his private business.

I can compare my friend's dad with my own dad. My dad often seemed frustrated and angry about work and finances. I knew it growing up, but it was not until I was older that I realized why. My dad would often come home with a scowl and rarely spoke of what he did at work. On the other hand, my friend's dad was almost always upbeat and full of energy and would constantly talk about what he was doing—oftentimes seeking input from anyone willing to listen. His son would joke that his dad spent his days meeting up with his "cronies." Several of these "cronies," really just other business owners and investors, would talk to me and encourage me to find my own path. They were engineers, Realtors, and other business owners, and all seemed happy, even thrilled, to share how they had become financially independent. My dad really did not have "work friends," and when I did meet them, they were very kind but seemed focused elsewhere, as though they were there for business and the socialization was a means to an end.

I cannot say anything negative about the folks my dad worked with—they were all kind, successful, and seemed really nice. But my mentor's rich friends, without exception, did not seem overly concerned about their money. They were all too busy talking about their next adventure, new product launch, or whatever else they were excited about. In contrast, my father's rich friends all seemed focused on getting whatever they were meeting for completed. It was a subtle difference, but I now see a world of difference between the two groups and have a better understanding of what was motivating them. It was not until my dad joined a small dinner group of successful businesspeople that included independent business owners that he even saw the difference. When he did, he realized something and immediately pushed to have me spend time with the independent business owners in the group.

It was the first time he ever said to me that he knew "what *not* to do" and wanted me to be around people who "knew what to do." My dad told me *not* to do as he had done and work for corporate America. He even said, "Toby, college isn't for everyone—you should open your own business." As if to try and convince me of this point, he introduced me to friends of his who had their own businesses. One of these friends owned a collection of franchises. One was a Subway, another was a Minute Lube, and he was constantly adding to his portfolio of franchises. He would occasionally meet me for lunch and give me advice. One thing he told me stuck with me more than anything else. I asked him what he liked best about what he did, and he replied in a way that, at the time, seemed odd. Now, thirty years later, it makes perfect sense to me. He answered by saying that if someone who worked for him was doing a good job, he loved being able to simply say, "Take your spouse to dinner on me—somewhere really nice, on me." It was not what I expected at the time, but now I get it.

Looking back through the lens of everything I have learned, I believe my dad was frustrated because he did not feel like he was in control. In his mind, his involvement with his job was negative because he felt that he was at the mercy of someone else. To top this off, he had a mortgage and a family to support. He must have felt imprisoned by his financial burden—like he would always be working in service of other people and his debt. He looked around and saw people who did not feel like they were carrying the same financial burden he was and did what any good father would do—he urged his kids to be free. He just did not know specific ways to help.

My friend's dad was the opposite. He had freedom. He seemed to have no real schedule or pressing obligations. He was financially independent, and whether he worked or not, money came in. So he did other things with his time. He ran for political office, flew around the country checking on his investments, and helped people start their own ventures. He encouraged others to be independent, and what was so interesting to me was that it did not matter if they worked for a *Fortune* 500 or were self-employed. He showed them how to create what is now commonly referred to as *passive income*. This is income that comes in whether you are sleeping or awake. You earn it whether you are in the office or on vacation. This kind of income survives you and takes care of those you leave behind and the organizations you care about.

The truth is that all of my mentors had one thing in common—they wanted freedom. Many had achieved it and quite deliberately maintained their freedom with simple philosophies on how to build wealth. If my dad were alive today, I would be able to tell him that his instincts were right—he was onto something—and that because of that I have been able to live with tremendous freedom. As for my friend's dad, I was able to talk to him before he passed and thank him. I will keep that conversation to myself but will say that even at the end, he went out on his terms and without an ounce of regret. He knew exactly what he had set up and was comfortable in the fact that it would continue.

Now imagine for a moment the frustration of working your tail off and still feeling completely boxed in and without control. Imagine a scenario in which no matter how hard you work, you still feel helpless. It has to be frustrating— maddening even. It is not something we would choose if we knew alternatives, but as is so often the case, financial burdens sneak up on us if we don't actively plan. We are tricked into golden cages—imprisoned by lifestyles we cannot afford and investments designed to erode our wealth. The cost is our freedom.

To get out of your cage or, better yet, to avoid it entirely, all you need is a methodology that you can use to keep you from getting tricked into doing the things that create financial imprisonment. It is not rocket science. It is actually painfully simple. But simple does not mean easy. For example, losing weight seems pretty straightforward: burn more calories than you consume. But losing weight isn't easy for most people. It takes self-discipline and conscious effort. Money is no different. The solution to avoid financial imprisonment is simple. In this book I am going to show you exactly how to do it—step-by-step—so you can avoid a life of financial service to others. But it will take effort on your part.

Whether you are rich or poor, an employee or self-employed, a college graduate or not, you have the same access to the tools the rich have been using for generations to create perpetual wealth for themselves and their families.

How do I know?

As a tax attorney, I have worked with tens of thousands of investors and have seen firsthand who makes money consistently and how they do it. It became obvious to me from working with their financial records who had to work for their money and who had money flowing in without working. Even better, I see their tax returns and know who has created actual wealth and who is just living a lavish lifestyle that is confused with actually being wealthy. Based on this experience, I have been able to drill down into the IRS data—data that is published every year—and discover the financial behaviors and patterns that are consistent with the wealthiest among us. The best part about it is that anyone can build perpetual wealth. *You* can—it is actually simple math that a fourth-grader would understand. The rest is just following the system and enjoying the results. Welcome to Infinity Investing.

The chapters are organized to guide you through the process. Chapter 1 is designed to help you understand what financial freedom means for you. I then introduce you to the startling concept of financial imprisonment in chapter 2. The fact is that most financial institutions limit your freedom to leverage your own money for their benefit. I'm going to be blunt. A lot of these institutions rip us off, and they do it because the law allows them to and, quite frankly, we do not know any better. We can easily fall victim to it over and over and over again, and in the meantime, we are left wondering where our money went and trying to figure out what happened to our retirement fund. When you actually start digging into these things, you'll realize just how systematically financial institutions behave to burden us with a yoke of debt that creates a lack of hope—especially for young people.

We're going to look at the number-one difference between the wealthy and the poor in chapter 3. Hint: It probably is not what you have been taught.

In Chapters 4 through 6, you will learn how to calculate something we call your income spread and find out why that matters. I describe how my approach is different from the traditional method and why the old way was simply institutional trickery. Once you understand this approach, I can show you how to convert old numbers into the new numbers to calculate your Infinity Plan.

In addition to studying clients who were successful in building wealth, I also examined the reasons other people were not successful because, as John Dewey said, "Failure is instructive." We can learn a lot from the financial mistakes of others. These failures tend to fall into three categories, and because they are predictable, they are avoidable. Chapters 7 and 8 identify these three losing bets (the Big Nos) that keep you in captivity and then examine what people are doing to break free. We will discuss the three things that they're doing to be successful. This is a universal truth. If you do what these folks are doing, you will join them. You will be in at least the top 20 percent of wealth holders and have a fighting chance to get in the top 2 percent, who are the multimillionaires in our society.

Do you realize that each of us is either a financial serf, apprentice, knight, or steward? In chapter 9 you will learn what those terms mean and where you fall. This might be difficult for you to hear, but it could reveal a financial blind spot you have and help you make adjustments to move up in your financial class status. Chapter 10 describes what we know about where the wealthy invest. Our research shows that if you follow the investment patterns of that group, chances are you can be wealthy too. You'll learn a unique investment strategy in chapter 11 to become something I call a Stock Market Landlord, and how to increase your financial class in chapter 12.

Again, this is not a get rich quick scheme. It is a long-range plan that, if followed, can create a legacy of wealth for you and future generations. Like any long-range plan, it starts with specific, immediate tactics to get you started. In chapter 13 I describe a ninety-day plan to begin to move the needle immediately on your financial class, and it all starts with taking one critical first step. Finally, I will show you the importance of accountability. One of the biggest barriers to success is trying to do this all yourself. An accountability group dramatically increases the odds of anyone reaching personal goals, whether they are fitness, diet, or financial goals.

Are you ready to take the first step toward your own Infinity Plan? Read on!

Chapter 1
The Meaning of Financial Freedom

David was a friend of mine in Seattle, and he was an old-time restaurateur who had managed to have a tremendous amount of success. I met David as he was shifting his goals from wanting to be rich to wanting to make a difference in people's lives. As part of his plan he had transitioned from the restaurant business to real estate. I met him while I was helping an elderly woman as her court-appointed guardian. I will call her Sue for purposes of this story.

Sue had some valuable real estate, and a neighbor was essentially trying to steal it from her. Sue had diminished capacity, and her neighbor knew that she wasn't making payments on her taxes for the property. He was contacting the county to see if they could negotiate for the back debt and foreclose on the properties. I was brought in because Sue was having a difficult time caring for herself. Her electricity had been turned off, and her houses were in such poor condition they were barely habitable. Instead of helping Sue, the neighbor saw it as a great way to get some prime Seattle property at foreclosure prices. Someone recommended David as a Realtor who would work on greatly reduced commissions to help people. As I got to know him, I found him to be an interesting guy. I learned that David had made a significant amount of money owning and operating restaurants in Seattle.

In getting to know him, I learned some important lessons from him. Number one, he told me that he didn't have any plans beyond making his restaurants successful. In other words, his goal was to hit a certain dollar figure, let's call it $1 million a year, in his restaurants. And he hadn't thought about much beyond that. He told me that when he had his first year of $1 million, it was probably the worst year of his life and he didn't know what to do. He did what so many people do when they start making money—he started spending it very irresponsibly. David got into drugs, alcohol, womanizing, you name it. If it was a bad habit, he partook. Let's just say David's life became a train wreck. Which brings us to lesson number two. David said that the financial saving grace during that entire period was that he had invested in assets in the form of real estate throughout Seattle. He said even when he managed to destroy his restaurants and was doing his best to make a mess out of his life, the real estate continued to support him and, as he put it, "bailed me out and saved my ass."

You see, even though David lost direction, he was able to eventually correct his trajectory. What fascinated me was that his new trajectory had nothing to do with restaurants. Rather, it was a commitment to serve other people, and his investments allowed him to make that shift. When I met him, he was older, wiser, and said he didn't miss the restaurant business. He loved real estate, and he loved helping people who had nobody else to turn to.

David helped me with Sue, and he did her a tremendous service. I stayed in touch with him for years after that. He was always tinkering in helping somebody out, and I was somewhat jealous. I was a professional, and I was working hard to establish myself. I worked a lot of hours and put myself through a lot to build up my practice. I couldn't help but be envious that David was so relaxed and seemed to be enjoying every minute of every day. To me it looked like David didn't have a care in the world other than how to help the next person.

I think what struck me most was how David described the point when he finally accomplished his earnings goal in his restaurant business and how quickly his life unraveled thereafter. Choosing a dollar amount—a financial goal—without purpose can lead to a devastating fall. It is kind of like climbing to the top of the mountain with no plans to get back down. As any accomplished mountaineer will tell you, when you summit, you are halfway there; you still have the second half of the trip, coming back down. Your plan needs to cover both the accumulation and the maintenance of wealth, and that requires exploration into your *purposes* for building wealth.

WHAT FINANCIAL FREEDOM MEANS FOR YOU

The fact that you are reading this book shows that you have a serious interest in controlling your own financial future. Congratulations. You have already separated yourself from the pack. Far too many people are content to move forward in their daily lives, completely unaware that they are imprisoned by a variety of financial institutions. You have made a life-changing decision by choosing to spend time learning about Infinity Investing, and you will never look at money the same way. This book will help you set a course for financial freedom by laying out a road map of clear, specific steps. It doesn't matter how old you are. Perhaps you are a twenty-year-old who is trying to make decisions about managing your money. Or maybe you are fifty years old and having an "Uh oh!" moment, realizing that you need to make financial changes for your immediate future. The purpose of this book is not to set unrealistic goals for younger readers or to make older readers feel guilty about what they have not yet done. The goal of the book is to help you.

This book is about being successful, and the information inside is based on my experience from over twenty years of advising wealthy clients. This is not a get rich quick scheme. It is a get rich slow approach based on data that I have collected from working with thousands of wealthy clients over the course of my career as an attorney, entrepreneur, and investor. In this work I discovered specific, repeated factors that differentiated people who became wealthy from those who did not—and those factors are almost certainly not what you think. It has nothing to do with how well you did in college or where you grew up. It comes down to mindset. Specifically, it comes down to your belief system and the degree to which you believe you can control your outcome.

FINANCIAL FREEDOM EXERCISE

Let's do a simple exercise to help you get some clarity on what financial freedom means for you. This exercise requires you to answer the following question: What comes to mind when I say, "What does financial freedom mean to you?" To help you answer this question, just stop, close your eyes, and consider that question, then write your answer down.

Let me offer my own reaction to that question as an example. For me, one thing financial freedom means is that I get to travel. So, for the purpose of this exercise, I would write that down.

The next step is to answer the following question: "Why is this important to me?"

So I would ask myself, "Why is it important to me to travel?" And I might write down that I want to experience the culture of my ancestors. You would continue repeating that same step until you arrived at the core of what it is that is motivating you—what it is that financial freedom really means to you, individually.

Using my example, I would ask myself, "Why is wanting to travel and experience the culture of my ancestors that important to me?" Then I write down that it would help me better understand my own values and family background. Then I just keep going deeper by asking myself that question

—"Why is it important to me?"

The idea here is to use this process to go deep in order to get clarity. Each time you ask yourself that question, it helps you get clearer and closer to the core values that will help you sustain your plan.

Some people call this getting clear on your "big why." And if you know why you're doing something, that's half the battle. You can focus in on it. You can write it on a piece of paper and say, "This is why this is important to me." Studies have shown your chances of achieving a goal go up 300 percent by this simple step of writing down the ultimate goal. Entire books have been written on the secret of achieving goals by identifying them and writing them down. For our purposes, we want to identify what is important to you so you can make it something that's important about you or, if you are a parent, so you can make it important to your family and you can say, "This is something that we are. This is something that we stand for."

Without this clarity, we are at the mercy of our whims. And trust me, you are being influenced—I would go so far as to say maybe even brainwashed— every day by the world of advertising. You are constantly being marketed to by everything you see on your phone and by everything you read on the internet. If you aren't actively aware of it, you're going to be led down the wrong path and away from your financial goals. Establish your own path based on the "big why" that you identified by answering the question about what financial freedom means to you.

Put another way, without something to guide us, we are a rudderless ship being cast about by the sea. You will drift on the currents and never reach your goals except by chance. By simply identifying what your goal is and why it is important, you can head in that direction with purpose. Don't worry, you can always tweak your goals, just as a ship headed to New York could alter course and head to Florida instead.

Once you know your goal and what it really means to be financially free for you, the next logical question is *"How much money do you need to get there?"*

We're going to use some specific metrics later in the book to determine just that. You can't just say, "Oh, I need a little bit of money." You need a dollar amount. You will need to do a traditional income statement or what the banks call an *income and expense statement.* In a business, it's known as a profit and loss statement. Banks would also request a personal balance sheet that shows your assets and liabilities, with the difference between the two known as your *net worth.* Banks use this whenever you apply for a loan. So no matter what world you're looking at, whether it's your company or whether it's you, you still use these categories. I'll break them down, and we will use these calculations to determine what you need to gain financial freedom.

So how do you define financial freedom? For you it might mean that you don't have to go to work anymore, or you can take a lower-paying or nonpaying job to do something you love. It might mean knowing that you always have a roof over your head. For some it means that you own your house and your cars outright. You don't have debt. That might be what you need. Other people might say they need to know that they have a certain amount of income coming in and are not reliant on others so that they can travel the world without worrying about paying bills. Still others might want to fund charities, do mission work, or give money to help others. There are no wrong answers, but we do need a destination. Think about what it means to you to be financially free, then we're going to calculate it. But before we do that, we have to talk about three very distinct lenses through which we consider what "enough" means.

NEEDS, WANTS, AND WISHES

Financial freedom for most people is greatly impacted by their understanding of the differences between needs, wants, and wishes. Let's look at each one of these.

Needs are the most basic of the three. If you think in terms of the services that FEMA provides for people during an emergency, these are the basic needs. People need water, shelter, food, and healthcare.

Wants are about how you prefer to live. Money, vacations, cars, and a house in a good neighborhood are all wants. Some people love to debate the difference between needs and wants, most often using the "it depends" argument. Most likely, the wants are how you are living right now. This is how you want to live without getting caught up in the financial aspects of life. You're spending without really much regard. Maybe you're carrying balances on credit cards. You have some debt, but you still go to the movies all the time. You travel and go on vacations. You want to do these things, but you don't need to. In other words, if you lost your job, you could cut most of these out if you had to. You have to be able to calculate these, and I'll show you how to do it.

Wishes are the ways you think about your life if everything were perfect. What would you like to be able to do? Maybe you wish you could own a second house in another part of the country. Maybe you wish you could participate in all of your church's mission trips. Whatever your wishes are, you need to be honest with yourself. You need to know exactly what your own needs, wants, and wishes are so you can calculate them. What do you need to have coming in to offset what it's going to cost? If your need is to not be homeless, then you need a roof over your head. You need basic transportation so you can take the kids to school and get yourself to your job. What are your basic needs? You need food on the table, but you want to go to the movies. You don't need to go to the movies, so we should know both numbers. Don't worry, I am not going to tell you to cut out your wants; in fact, I am going to calculate something called your *Infinity Net Worth* based on your wants. It is important to know your needs so we know when we have met them. There is nothing worse than seeing someone who had their needs met be led backward by an overzealous financial planner who "unretires" his client because he had no clue that their needs were already met and continued down a more aggressive approach to planning because he was ignorant. From now on you will know your numbers and you will lead your own plan.

It all comes down to knowing four simple financial categories:

- Income
- Expenses
- Assets
- Liabilities

In the next chapter, I'm going to show why depending on our financial institutions for our investment strategy can work against us. It will become clear as we do the calculations, but you need to know why there is such a disconnect between the average American and the financial institutions who are supposed to serve them.

Chapter 2
How Financial Imprisonment Works

Mary was a retired teacher. Her husband had passed several years before, and she spent her days meeting with her friends and enjoying her garden. She loved her home; it held so many memories for her and felt like a continuing connection with her late husband. Mary felt financially secure, but she always wondered if she really knew enough about managing her money in retirement. One of her friends had told her about a financial planner; we'll call him Allen. Allen was a very successful planner. He had great suits, impeccable hair, and he seemed to really know what he was doing. Mary made an appointment with Allen and met him in his impressive office. The carpets and art were beautiful, and when Allen sat at his big, gleaming cherry desk in the middle of his office, he had a presidential air.

Mary was impressed. Allen asked Mary what she needed and what her lifestyle was like. He did what most responsible financial planners would do, which is to try to get an idea of what the client is spending. Allen created a chart for Mary showing her spend down. The idea was that she would live off of 4 percent of her portfolio every year for the foreseeable future. At that rate her money would not run out unless she lived well beyond a hundred years old. And Mary felt very comfortable. She moved her accounts over to this advisor, and she moved her deceased husband's retirement accounts as well.

She maintained a small amount in her teacher's union retirement plan, and

Allen began handling her account. She would receive statements periodically from Allen, as well as a birthday and Christmas cards. Otherwise, she never heard a word from Allen. She would reach out about once a year to seek assurances that her portfolio was balanced. Allen would respond that everything was in accordance with standards. He told her not to worry, that she was in great shape for meeting her needs.

And then the market crashed. Mary was shocked to see her accounts lose more than a third of their value. She called up in a frazzled state and wanted to talk to Allen. Allen said to relax and that he would reposition her portfolio and reassured her that because of the planning he had done with her, she was in good shape to weather the storm. Mary had her doubts, so she scheduled a meeting with Allen to discuss specific steps. As she sat with Allen, he talked about things like allocation and diversification and all the mutual funds that he had put her in and how she just needed to wait for the market to correct and it would come back. But Mary indicated that she needed those funds to live off of, and selling them now to turn them into cash so that she could live off of them would cost her significantly because the market was hitting the bottom.

Allen reminded her that she had other sources of income, like Social Security benefits and a teacher's pension, that she could live off of so that she wouldn't have to sell any of her holdings. Mary added everything up and realized she still had a shortfall. In one fell swoop, she had lost nearly a third of her savings. And she was not happy about it. Allen maintained that the investments he had put her in were suitable for her and were risk appropriate.

But Mary decided to get a second opinion and took her portfolio to a certified financial planner whom we will call Cindy. Cindy analyzed Mary's information and quickly saw that even though she had multiple mutual funds, many of those mutual funds contained the same underlying investments. In short, fund one may have had a position of 10 percent in XYZ Corporation and fund two may have had a 20 percent interest in XYZ Corporation— meaning even though Mary thought she was diversified in multiple companies, she was aggressively exposed to one company's fortunes.

Cindy also put the profile through an analyzer that rated risk exposure and found that Mary was not in a conservative portfolio as Allen had told her but rather was in an aggressive, tech-heavy portfolio—meaning she needed those companies to do well for her to make money. And the only reason the balances in her portfolio looked high was because those stocks were in demand at the time. And as soon as the demand went away, the stocks dropped and she had no real assets in her portfolio.

Mary was shocked. She had done everything right. She knew her own limits and engaged a financial planner. She laid out exactly what she needed to live off of. And she expected the financial planner to create a portfolio for her that would weather downturns. Now she was discovering that the opposite was actually true. Mary realized that she would have no other option but to sell her home and downsize to allow her to adjust her standard of living so that she did not have to liquidate her portfolio when it was down. And she learned a very important lesson. It was ultimately her responsibility to ensure that her plan suited her needs. Cindy explained what it meant to have a fiduciary responsibility to somebody versus using suitability standards. Mary's eyes were now wide open.

THE SECRET ABOUT FINANCIAL INSTITUTIONS

Many financial institutions don't have your best interest in mind. If you don't believe me, consider this recent example: a high-level employee at Morgan Stanley discovered a shocking truth about his own company. After carefully scrutinizing the investment products included in the Morgan Stanley employees' retirement plan, he realized it included many of the expensive, underperforming, and high management fee products he sold daily to clients. According to the Morgan Stanley employee, investing in these funds cost Morgan Stanley employees millions of dollars in lost retirement savings. Why would Morgan Stanley do this? Because by buying the Morgan Stanley funds, it provided significant revenue and profits for Morgan Stanley even as it compromised the value of their own employees' retirement funds. The high-level Morgan Stanley employee ended up being the lead plaintiff when a group of Morgan Stanley employees brought a class action suit against their employer. Basically, the Morgan Stanley employees, many of whom sold Morgan Stanley products to consumers, thought so little of the products they sold that they sued because their employer held the very same products in the company retirement account. Sounds crazy, but it is 100 percent true.

It isn't just Morgan Stanley. Unfortunately, there are many other examples. The *Wall Street Journal* reported on a lawsuit brought by Florida-based teachers against their union.[1] The union urged members to buy their retirement investments through a firm owned by the union. They didn't reveal to the teachers that the fund had higher fees and would translate to a smaller nest egg when the teachers retired. This should be a sobering example for all readers about the way many financial institutions operate.

Financial imprisonment is a real thing, and you are going to learn what it means in this chapter. World history shows many examples of abuses that took place by people who controlled information. For example, in certain medieval churches, the Bibles were in Latin and it was illegal for a commoner to learn Latin. That meant that the average person had to go to somebody who could interpret the content for them—often in a way that benefited the interpreter. They could say something like, "The Bible says you have to pay me money, and then you can go to heaven."

In some cases, entire classes of people were controlled by what they were allowed to know or learn. In many cases education was permitted only when it was absolutely required to perform one's job. They were only allowed to read, do math, or write if it contributed to the welfare of the ruling class. In other words, they were deliberately keeping them in the dark—and that's how financial imprisonment works. Financial institutions try to keep us in the dark, and in this book I shine a light on it so you can avoid being held captive by banks and brokerage houses.

This is evident in the United States as well. When a very small percentage of people control a huge percentage of the wealth, it means that the rest of us are almost always working on their behalf. In the financial world, there are the governors and there are the captives. The governors are in control, and the captives have to do things for them. How? Financial imprisonment is sustained as a result of the practical impact of debt. Debt is the mechanism by which they can control you. Debt is how they get you to go to work every day for somebody else. Debt is how you wake up at sixty and realize you are literally working to pay your living expenses and the rest of your money is going to pay interest on debts with little to no money put aside for retirement.

By the way, you can be self-employed and still be working for somebody else. Who owns your house? Chances are it's a bank or mortgage company. If you own your house outright, then you know that feeling of a little bit of freedom. It feels good because you realize you're not working for somebody else. If you don't own your own house or if you have a mortgage on it, and especially if you went through the great recession, you realize how destructive it can be to have debt on something that you thought was an asset. My position is that a home with a mortgage is not an asset. You're actually buying a liability (your house) with a liability (your mortgage loan), which is what causes so much pain. We're going to explore what the practical impact of this can be. I'm going to show you the statistics, and it will probably be as eye-opening for you as it was for me.

THE SOCIAL SECURITY MYTH

Let's dive right in and look at some stats. Studies have shown that about 42 percent of Americans are going to retire broke, with less than $10,000. They are, in essence, on welfare. You might want to argue by saying, "Hey, I've been paying into Social Security all these years." Sorry. That makes you dependent on somebody else determining how much you're going to receive, and in a stroke of a pen, it could go away. I'm not a big fan of relying on public programs. No offense to public programs, but they should serve as a safety net, not a retirement plan. When Social Security was created, it was intended to provide coverage for people who outlived the normal life expectancy at that time. The projection was that most people would only need this coverage for about a two-year span. In fact, according to the Social Security Administration website, the average life expectancy of men in the United States when Social Security was enacted was fifty-eight years old.

If it is a true safety net, it should be there simply to cover you if you live too long. Nowadays people are relying on it to actually cover their retirement. You absolutely have to be accountable to yourself, and the essential philosophy of Infinity Investing is doing just that. We have to have money coming in whether we're working or not. You might argue, "Hey, if I put my time in, I'm entitled to Social Security." Maybe you are, maybe that's an income source that you think you can count on, but I'm not going to. I'm going to look at assets that are producing income, and Social Security is just a safety net. I might still be receiving it, but I'm not going to count it toward my calculations because it's not something that's in my control. Somebody else could take it away.

BARRIERS TO RETIREMENT SAVINGS

According to a recent report from the US Government Accountability Office, half of Americans approaching retirement have nothing saved in a 401(k) or other individual account.[2] Why aren't Americans saving for retirement? Well, let's face it, many of us live pretty lavish lifestyles. Almost everybody walks around with a mobile phone, yet so many of us don't have enough money to save for our retirement. It's because we don't understand the importance of it, or, even if we do understand why it is important, we don't make it a priority.

I am an attorney by trade, so I'm going to be the first one to tell you, stuff happens. I do tax protection for estate planning, and I know things can come up that you don't plan for. That's why an important part of any financial plan includes having an emergency fund, but it's not what we use as a calculation for developing a plan of continuous wealth. You have to build in protection separately. Let's use health insurance as an example. If I have a catastrophic illness and I don't have health insurance, it's going to be a devastating situation for me financially. So I'm going to mitigate that risk by having health insurance. You could use a similar example when it comes to driving a car. There's a good chance you'll never have a car accident or if you do, it will be minor. But if you do have a serious accident that involves injury or death and you get hounded by an ambulance-chaser who tries to extort money out of you, you can reduce your risk by having insurance. This also applies to homeowner's insurance and life insurance. You should absolutely, positively, have some sort of life insurance. Consider the statistics. If you live to be over sixty, you have more than a 50 percent risk of having to incur long-term care expenses—and the average cost is over $200,000. If you know that you are statistically at 50 percent risk for something, you should mitigate that risk. In this case it would involve having long-term care insurance.

When I hear somebody say, "I don't have enough money," I am skeptical.

I can tell you from my experience in criminal court, if a judge offers a suspect the option to leave jail by paying bail, people always manage to find money. Almost nobody stayed in jail—I don't care what their financial position was. Somehow, if there's a big enough need, people find the money. Sometimes it's just not a big enough priority to start saving for retirement because you would rather do other things. You'd rather go to the movies, you'd rather go out to eat twice, three times a week instead of cutting back and making it a priority. If you made retirement saving a priority and you treated it like a bill, then you could do it. This requires what I like to call a "checkup from the neck up." It requires that you look at your own mindset instead of external circumstances you blame for your not having enough money.

Other excuses I hear include "My job doesn't offer a retirement plan." That's abdicating your responsibility for yourself to somebody else. Another excuse I hear is "I'm prioritizing paying down debt before I build up my asset base." Well, that's one that I understand. I would still say you can do both. Most of the excuses I hear are a bunch of hooey. I'm not saying that there isn't a small minority of people that can't possibly save for retirement. But because you are reading this book, that isn't you. You can start retirement savings today or tomorrow. Somehow, some way, you are going to start. I don't care if it's only ten dollars—you're going to start it. Once you do it, once you build that habit and you treat it like a bill over time, statistically speaking that will build to over $1 million at some point in the future. It's just math.

THE BURDEN OF DEBT

If we look back to the period from 2000 to 2007, the economy really heated up. Then the great recession hit, and the wheels started to come off. An important part of this story involves taking into consideration what happened with student debt. Since the start of the great recession, student debt has skyrocketed. According to the board of governors of the Federal Reserve system, during this time student debt has more than tripled.

Here is where things went wrong for a lot of people. People were losing their jobs, and one of the popular remedies being thrown out into the discussion was "Go back to school, learn a new trade, switch career fields, or get an MBA!" The problem was that people didn't have jobs, so they didn't have the money to pay for tuition. They had to borrow, which put them further in debt without any income coming in while they were back in school.

It is compelling to compare student debt with credit card debt during the great recession. Credit card debt dropped during much of the time, while student debt did the opposite. What made matters so much worse (and is a dirty secret of debt in our country) is that you can't get rid of student debt the way you can get rid of other kinds of debt.

Unlike in the case of student debt, you could max out your credit cards by going to Las Vegas and having a bender. You could gamble up a storm, have a blowout party weekend, spend all kinds of money, and put it all on your credit card. Then, if your credit card debt is below $50,000, you can bankrupt that credit card. However, if you have a $50,000 student debt, you can't bankrupt that debt. Sure, some politicians talk about forgiving student debt, but so far it is just talk. There are some programs out there that can forgive certain amounts of student debt for teaching or public service, but you cannot bankrupt it away. That's with you forever.

THE IMPACT OF DEBT ON HOME OWNERSHIP

Now the dominos start to fall. Student debt impacts homeownership rates. Student debt goes up, and homeownership gets pushed down, so our young people can't afford to buy a home; they have to rent.

Let's flip this around. This means you have a lot of people looking for houses to rent, which creates a need in the marketplace. This means you should be a landlord. You might think that's crazy—a real leap of logic. But the stats as reported by the *Wall Street Journal* and The Urban Institute show that homeownership among young people is at its lowest point in three generations. The young are renting. Period. What does that tell you? It tells me that debt has caused a severe situation. Student debt has a direct correlation to homeownership rates going down. If that's not financial imprisonment, then I don't know what is. They just forced you to become somebody who leases property from somebody else. I don't know what else to call that. Sorry, if you are renting because you have to, you're a captive.

THE IMPORTANCE OF A FIDUCIARY

Let's consider where our financial advice is coming from. Whom are we listening to? Who is supposed to be advising us? I'm going to introduce you to a guy named Bob who owns a butcher shop in your neighborhood. You've known Bob for years, and you consider him a friend. You walk into his shop, and Bob smiles, says hello, and asks about your kids. He asks you how he can help you today, and you say, "Hey, Bob, I am so tired of planning our meals; can you help me figure out our dinner menu for next week?" Eager to help, Bob suggests that on Monday you should have the nice veal he just got in. Tuesday you should have chicken. Wednesday would be good for a rib roast. Thursday should be pork chop night, and for Friday, he has a very beautiful sirloin that would be a big hit with the family. What is Bob not going to tell you to eat for dinner? Bob is not going to tell you to eat more fish and leafy vegetables. He's not going to send you down to the farmer's market for fresh fruit. He's not going to say, "Cut back your red meat intake. It's really not good for you to eat too much of what I sell." Wait a minute, I thought Bob was your friend. Why is he giving you bad advice? Because Bob is a butcher. His business is selling meat. He makes his money by selling meat. He is looking out for his best interest, not yours.

It's not just Bob. If you go to the Toyota dealership and ask, "What's the best car for me?" they will show you the top of the line Toyota on the lot. Go to a Cadillac dealership, and they will recommend that you buy a Cadillac. Bob the butcher, the Cadillac dealer, and the Toyota dealer are businesspeople. They are not required to look out for your best interest.

You are a bit rattled after your visit to Bob, and you realize you should take more responsibility for your family's good health, so you go talk to a nutritionist named Dr. Mary and you ask her, "What should our family eat for dinner?" And Dr. Mary makes a meal plan centered on eating a balanced diet of whole grains, vegetables, and fish. Notice she's not recommending veal. She's not selling you anything. She is what is called a *fiduciary*. This word just might be the most important word in this book. A fiduciary puts your needs before their own.

The problem is that 90 percent of Americans think that their financial planner is a fiduciary when they're not. When you go into the bank and ask them what to invest in, they are likely going to sell you whatever investment products they have that make them the most money. That is their business model. They're not necessarily going to do what's in your best interest because they are not required to. If you go into a bank and walk up to the CD desk, they're going to sell you a CD. If you go to a brokerage house, they're going to sell you a bunch of equities. I've seen very wealthy people lose their money in the markets because they were sold what a brokerage wanted to sell them. Then the broker churned their account, buying and selling equities because that is how brokerages make money. It is their business model. They are not a fiduciary.

And before you think I am exaggerating, let's go back to the Morgan Stanley lawsuit that I described at the beginning of the chapter. Morgan Stanley invested the retirement funds in a way that provided significant revenue and profits to Morgan Stanley, but, as the employees complained, it did not result in a retirement portfolio that was in the best interest of the employee. Morgan Stanley did not act as a fiduciary. This is very important because the fiduciary requirement demands that the retirement account manager act in the best interest of the participant. Without the fiduciary responsibility, they could just operate under what is called a *suitability standard*.

Let me explain the difference in plain English by using the car analogy again. Let's say you have a family of four and you walk into a Chevrolet dealership and say, "I need transportation for my family." They could sell you two souped-up Corvettes. They might say, "Hey, you have four people. Mom and Dad could each drive one car, and you can put one kid with each of you in the other passenger seat." Technically, that option meets the suitability standard because it does provide transportation for a family of four. Is that option in the best interest of your family? Of course not. A much more logical, less expensive, and safer option for the family is an SUV or a minivan. That would be in the family's best interest. If the Chevrolet dealer operated under a suitability standard, they could sell you the Corvettes and make a lot of money because technically the two-Corvette option meets the suitability standards for transportation for a family of four. If they had a fiduciary responsibility to your family, they would be required to sell you the product that is in your best interest—not theirs. That's what a fiduciary is required to do. Otherwise the Chevy dealer can sell you Corvettes and the banker can sell you mutual funds.

THE MUTUAL FUND MYTH

So how does the fiduciary obligation impact mutual fund management? Let's jump into the actual numbers behind a mutual fund. This isn't just my opinion; it is what *Forbes* calls the real cost of mutual funds and retirements.[3] The reason I mention it here is because what fund managers are required to disclose to you is not the actual expense. The way to calculate the actual cost is simple. You look at what you had at the beginning of the year and compare it to what you have at the end of the year. Did it go up in value or did it go down? That will tell you whether or not you actually had a return. Sounds simple, right?

Let's say you had $100,000 in a mutual fund account and your fund advisory says, "Hey, we had a 7 percent gain this year." You would probably expect to have $107,000 in your mutual fund balance. But when you look at your statement, you see that you have $102,000 in your account. That math is pretty simple; your return was only 2 percent. Your broker can technically tell you it is a 7 percent return because legally they're not required to disclose all of the expenses that they charge. The only way you can figure out what it actually costs is by doing the math and calculating what the tax costs and other fees are on these mutual funds. That's the reason I'm not a big fan of mutual funds. They are very expensive.

Why is that the case? Because there are hidden fees associated with mutual fund accounts that you don't have to deal with in other kinds of investments. Mutual funds have an expense ratio. They contain transaction costs, and brokerage commissions are part of the transaction costs, as are market impact report fees and data spread costs. Also, you're usually paying taxes as you go since the fund is reporting them. Because even though it's a mutual fund, it's not a tax deferred vehicle; you may be paying taxes on somebody else's money as a result. You have what is called *cash drag* costs, which means they have to have a certain amount of liquidity. If you have a mutual fund with $10 million in it, they're probably keeping $500,000 liquid. As a result, it's not $10 million that's invested in the market; it's $9.5 million, and that cash drag ends up being close to 1 percent.

There is also something called *soft dollar cost*, which is more difficult to calculate. You have to reverse engineer these to figure out what the actual cost is. An example of soft dollar cost is when a brokerage has multiple mutual funds and they redirect the costs. For example, mutual fund X is a fund designed for select heavy-hitter investors. The brokers will want to do a lot of research to carefully populate that fund, so they purchase a bunch of research data from other sources. Then there's mutual fund Y, which is a larger, public fund that caters to what the fund managers consider lower-level clients. The brokers may decide to charge all the fund X research against fund Y. As an investor in fund Y, you are paying what they call soft dollar. You are paying for research that benefits somebody else. The mutual fund picks up the cost, and then the firm has access to that data. They're using it for the benefit of others, but you're the one paying for it.

There are advisory fees as well. When you buy a mutual fund, an institution is getting paid. It might be Wells Fargo or another institution that's serving as an advisor. You add all those things up and the total costs on that cash drag and everything else is right around 4 percent. The soft dollar advisory fees push it closer to a 5.8 percent. Last year the S&P index recorded a 7 percent return, and when you adjust for inflation, it might even be closer to 9 percent. When you subtract 5.8 percent for all of the fees you are being charged, all of a sudden that return doesn't look so great.

I once made this presentation to a large group. Afterward one participant went back and looked at the stocks and mutual funds that they had in their retirement fund. The fund published a return rate close to 7 percent. But upon closer inspection, he discovered that the fund expenses were about 5 percent. The actual amount he was receiving was 2 percent. They guy was shocked.

I have had people in the audience argue with me and say, "I have fifty thousand dollars in a mutual fund." And I'll say, "What is the value at the end of the year?" The balance at the end of the year is below $50,000, and they try to convince me that they had a 5 percent or 6 percent positive result for the year. I have to say "That's nonsensical. Your numbers tell me something very different." I don't care what a brokerage claims about performance. I only care about how much cash is actually in my account—and so should you.

WHO IS WORKING FOR WHOM?

In the cases I described, who is working for whom? When you consider the impact of these fees year over the year, you'll realize that it is you who is working for them. Assume that you have a mutual fund account and each year you make a $10,000 contribution and you had 7 percent growth. You did that for thirty years. You were growing it at 7 percent and paid management costs at 4.8 percent.

Your direct contribution to this fund over thirty years is $300,000, and your actual balance is going to be about $415,000. You may say, "Fantastic! That's a lot of money." But you could avoid those fees by investing the same amount on your own. If you just dropped those payments in an S&P exchange-traded fund, for example, and it just returned what the market made, you would have $1,020,000. Instead you invested in a mutual fund and you lost $605,000 to Wall Street. Who made more off of your money, you or Wall Street? You have a $415,000 account. Wall Street made $605,000. Who is working for whom?

What if we reduced the management cost from the 4.8 percent down to 2 percent? The good news is your balance would now be about $688,000. The bad news is you still paid Wall Street $332,000. Sure, it's only 2 percent, but that is an awful lot of money to be paying some brokerage house. Again, you have to ask yourself, whose best interest do they have in mind? Who is working for whom here?

Using the data for management fee rates from the SEC and a study by Personal Capital, if you have a $500,000 brokerage account and you let it sit there for thirty years, Merrill Lynch will make almost a million dollars off your money.[4] The lowest one is USAA, and they make about half a million. So why do you want to be buying these products at all?

A mutual fund is just a bucket of stocks. In fact, what's weird is you often don't really know what's in them. So if I ask you why you would buy a mutual fund at all, you will probably say that you do it to keep a diversified portfolio of stocks. In fact, to be as diversified as you can, you bought two separate mutual funds. The problem is, each of those mutual funds may have 30 percent of their position in one particular company and you don't know it. You're thinking you're diversified, and what you really did is put yourself squarely at risk.

The alternative to that is something called an *ETF* or an *exchange-traded fund*, which is also just a bunch of stocks, but you buy one share of an ETF and within that share you own a small piece of a whole bunch of these companies. So I could buy one share of a bond ETF and I have five thousand bonds. I could buy one share of an ETF that's in the energy sector, for example, and now I have every company that's in that sector. There might be ten companies or four hundred companies in there. I pick a specific type of fund where I like the portfolio and the return it is earning and I only have one cost, which is the transaction cost.

Does it make a difference to your portfolio? You better believe it does.

Let's say you had $10,000 that you invested. If you're paying 5 percent of that $10,000 in fees, that adds up to $500 every year. If I buy those same companies in an ETF, I pay about two bucks.

FUNDS UNDER THE MICROSCOPE

Let's take a look at a real-world example. For more than forty years, my colleague David McShane has been analyzing brokerage fund accounts with a fine-toothed comb. One of our clients held a portfolio worth $398,000. David broke down what the undisclosed fees in that account were. Now he could see the management fees, the expense ratios, and all of the nondisclosed costs on all of these different securities funds.

His research showed a wide spread of management fees, from an outrageous high of 14 percent all the way down to one fund that charged 1.8 percent. The lowest one was a Goldman Sachs SPDR, which means you're paying almost 2 percent on something that you could just buy for no fee. The average of the fees across the group of twenty-four funds that David McShane researched was 4.29 percent. If you managed your portfolio yourself and all you did was buy your own ETFs containing the same companies, your fees would go from $17,000 to about a thousand bucks. You would literally be saving $16,000 a year on a $400,000 portfolio.

The purpose of all of this is to show you how much of your money is disappearing when you just do what your broker says so that they can maximize the amount of money you are earning for them. Again, I ask you, who is working for whom? I want you to think about this: *you take 100 percent of the risk, but you are receiving less than half of the return.* When you own a regular mutual fund, you are quite literally giving somewhere in the range of 70 percent of it to somebody else, but you have 100 percent of the risk. This makes no sense.

Chapter 3

The Number-One Difference between the Wealthy and the Poor

When I went through law school, I worked as a tutor in the law school's Academic Research Center, which focused on providing access to the legal profession for diverse and nontraditional students. One of the things we looked at was what kept certain groups down in the dirt while other groups thrived. It wasn't where they came from. More often than not, success was about *empowerment*—success hinges on *empowering* people who are traditionally disenfranchised from entering the legal profession, and the program has been an amazing success for decades.

Looking at economic success actually mirrors what I found to be the case in the Academic Research Center. Based on what I have seen, a group could be located in a depressed region with a bad government and somehow still be successful generationally. They would consistently pull themselves up out of whatever difficult situation they might have been in, whether it was racial prejudice, ethnic persecution, or some other life event that caused economic suffering. Meanwhile, another group might be given every opportunity to succeed, or at least the same opportunity as a successful group, yet remain in generational poverty. So what was the difference between the two groups?

The answer can be somewhat complex, in that it has to take into account that success requires people to collaborate with others to take advantage of available resources as they navigate the challenges they encounter. In other words, the individuals who succeed almost always find ways to leverage their way out of whatever situation they find themselves in. However, no matter what study you read, the same trends repeat over and over and ultimately boil down to one thing—what I call *the checkup from the neck up.*

It comes down to mindset and a sense of power and self-worth. Unsuccessful people didn't necessarily have a lack of resources. Rather, people with a certain mindset lacked resourcefulness. They didn't believe that they could actually create their own destiny. So the ultimate trait that separates groups who are almost constantly successful over time is their belief system. I'm going to explain how that works.

There is a significant mindset difference between those who have wealth and those who do not have wealth called *locus of control.* This is the belief that you actually have the ability to control your own outcomes. People with an *external locus of control* act in response to external circumstances. They have a mindset that whatever happens to them in life is a result of factors out of their control. People with an *internal locus of control* tend to believe that their life results are a result of their own attitude and abilities. They believe they have *agency* over their financial outcomes. This can be a powerful self-fulfilling prophecy. If you believe you have no control, chances are that you are not going to be successful. But here's the good news. If you believe you do have control, the odds are much greater that you will be successful.

The people who are economically successful—and especially those families with multigenerational success—have taken the time to learn how to work successfully with money. That's what you're doing now by reading this book. You can now start to see the difference in locus of control. I want you to know that you can control your money. You don't have to let other people and external circumstances control you.

COMMON MONEY MYTHS

Managing your financial life comes down to your belief system. It's complicated because whether we realize it or not, we're being programmed about money from an early age. Let's consider some of the common beliefs that get programmed into us from the time we are little kids. Are any of these familiar to you?

- Money doesn't grow on trees.
- It takes money to make money.
- There are two kinds of people, the haves and the have-nots.
- In the game of life, there must be winners and losers.

These are all false, and they originate from a scarcity mentality. The opposite of scarcity is abundance—believing that the pie is infinitely growable. It is the belief that there is enough for everybody, that we can provide food and shelter and water and great housing for every human being that walks this planet and any future generations. Scarcity is the belief that there are truly limited resources and that you have to get yours at the expense of someone else—if you eat, someone else will go hungry. It is grounded in fear and negativity and is exactly what keeps people impoverished when they have the resources and ability to have wealth.

Where do these negative, scarcity-based beliefs come from? Sources include parents, friends, schools, bosses, and the media. They're all around us, and it's easy for us to buy into them. If we don't combat them, they will impact our belief system. Again, what it really boils down to is one word: mindset. You are in complete control of your mindset. You can decide, "Hey, I have control over money. I'm a millionaire. I have agency and control."

I have friends that have made hundreds of millions, lost hundreds of millions, then made them back again because of their mindset and strong internal locus of control. You can think of this as a kind of thermostat. Before he became a president, I would use Donald Trump as an example. Would he be happy making $100,000 a year? Hardly. He thinks in terms of hundreds of millions. His thermostat is set that high. By comparison, some people are happy just to make an extra thousand bucks. Their thermostat is set that low.

Because mindset is an internal process, we can control it. Once we control our mindset, then we can control our beliefs. If I believe that the world has lots of opportunity and that it's up to me to go out and take advantage of those opportunities that I can control, then those opportunities are going to show up because I'm going to be open to them. I'm going to be looking for them and will notice them when they appear.

Here's an example of how that works. Think about the last time you decided that you were going to buy a certain kind of car. Let's say you decided to buy, just for example, a Honda Pilot. From that moment on, you noticed that Pilots were all over the place. Every other car you passed on the highway seemed like it was a Honda Pilot. Did Pilots suddenly outsell every other car over the course of a few weeks? Hardly. This particular mental effect is known as the Baader-Meinhof phenomenon. It's because you have opened your mind up to that Honda Pilot and your brain is paying selective attention to what is going on around you. On long family car trips when I was a kid, we used to play a game called Slug Bug. If you were the first to see a Volkswagen Beetle, you got to slug your brother or sister on the arm. The moment you open your mind to noticing something, you see that thing all over the place. Otherwise you arrive at the Grand Canyon with bruised arms.

That's your mindset playing out in your behaviors, but you can use it to your advantage. All you did is you changed your mindset and then suddenly

—"Hey, there are tons of Honda Pilots on the road." That's now your belief. Why? Because your mindset was that you were going to start looking for them. It can work the same way with your finances: if you say, "Hey, there are economic opportunities out there" and you believe it, guess what you start finding? You notice economic opportunities all over the place. They're everywhere. You have every ability to become wealthy if you want to, and you can start that process right now.

Once your mindset is "I can do it. I can start building up different sources of income. I can get to a point in my life where I don't have to work," you then start to believe it because it's true for you in your new worldview. Once your mind says, "This is an opportunity," that impacts your beliefs and that controls your behaviors. Once you realize that what you're believing is true, your behaviors will shift. Once you realize there are economic opportunities, you will start putting some money aside to take advantage of them. Once you believe that building up a portfolio will allow you to retire early and you don't have to work anymore, you are a volunteer, even if you are still getting a paycheck. Your behavior becomes very different, and you start becoming a very dedicated saver and a prolific investor. You will be investing all the time because you believe that you will be financially free as a result. When you add your mindset, beliefs, and behavior together, that's where you get these results. I guarantee it.

It doesn't happen overnight, but it's mathematically guaranteed that if you save money and you invest in high-value, income-producing investments, then you will be financially free at some point. Period. It's mathematically certain. Say to yourself, "I control this. My mindset comes from me." Just keep repeating it. "My mindset comes from me. My beliefs come from that mindset, and my behaviors come from my beliefs." Focus on your internal locus of control. "I have taken the time to learn how to work successfully with money. I do not let money control me." Just repeat it. "My money works for me. I tell it what to do."

CONVENTIONAL WISDOM ISN'T ALWAYS WISE

Let me offer a personal example. I moved to Las Vegas right at the end of 2007. You might remember that was right before the market crash that started the great recession. The Las Vegas market was hit particularly hard, losing 75 percent of its property values. At the time I was investigating different neighborhoods to find a good school district for my daughter—doing that thing that parents do. I'm convinced that when trying to find the right neighborhood, it's more about the community than about the school. Even if you homeschool, it's about the community, and it's about the people that you interact with.

As a result, I wanted to be in the kind of community that valued education. The problem was, to be in the neighborhood I wanted, the houses were crazy expensive because Vegas real estate prices at that time were off the charts. I was clear that I didn't want to buy one of these overpriced houses. I would have to put a lot of money down to buy a house. Instead, I could take that money and invest it in some rental properties on the other side of town to produce income. There were some awesome working-class neighborhoods, and I knew that was the part of town where I wanted to own. I could rent out houses over there due to high demand and lower cost of entry for me, so I bought a few houses that generated rental income for me.

Then, instead of buying a house in that crazy-expensive neighborhood where we wanted to live, I found a house to rent for my family. At the beginning of this chapter, I listed some of the common myths we are told about money that worm their way into our minds. Another one is that you should always buy a house as your primary residence. This isn't always true.

I was able to rent the house for a song because people were building big houses on speculation and there was no rental market to back it up. People were building or buying houses purely on hype, assuming their equity would continue to skyrocket, and because of the oversupply of high-end houses, rental costs were a steal.

What happened to the value of the house that we were renting? In the crash it lost more than half of its value, but the rent I paid stayed the same. What happened to the income I was making from the rental houses I owned? My rents remained steady throughout the recession, so I had rental properties paying for the house I lived in. Once the market recovered, I realized that for the same price I could rent for, I could probably go out and buy something. It's a wash. I didn't really care. I knew what my overhead was going to be on a monthly basis. I said, "Here's how much I'll allocate to cover shelter," and that's what I spent. If I could buy a house for it, great. If I could rent a house for it, great. It didn't really matter to me because I look at a house a little differently. I don't look at it as an asset. I look at it as a liability.

I had control of my money; it didn't have control of me. I didn't buy into the popular mantra that you're successful only if you're a homeowner (with a mortgage to go along with it). I want to own my house outright. Maybe I don't want to have a bunch of mortgage payments or if I do, I want to make sure that money is doing something else that's earning me more than what it's costing me. I needed to provide myself and my family with shelter in a good area. Did I provide that? Yes. Did I live in a great neighborhood? Yes. Did I get hit by the economic downturn like my neighbors? No. I had rental properties that paid me the same rent no matter what and helped cover my own rental expenses to live where I wanted.

It all comes down to a mindset of internal locus of control. It's just believing that you have control of it. In my example I had control of it. If I had listened to everybody else, I would've bought a house and I would've lost a ton of money. It's just making sure that your mindset's right.

MINDSET AS THE STARTING POINT

If you take nothing else from this chapter, then simply walk away with this affirmation, which you should repeat: "I believe that I control my money. My money does not control me." The number-one difference between the rich and the poor is the locus of control. The poor do not believe they have control over money. The poor often have a victim mindset. I've known people who have lost everything and built it right back up. They looked at their financial situation as a challenge, and they knew they had control over it. You have control over yours.

You will probably have setbacks. Most of us do. The world's full of them. It's also full of people who have come back from bankruptcy, some of them household names like Walt Disney, Elton John, and Donald Trump, to name a few. 3M was a bankrupt mine before it got started. Warren Buffett took advantage of a company that was in dire financial straits, and that's where Berkshire Hathaway came from.

You have control over money. At a very personal level, you can choose what to do with the money. I know it doesn't always feel that way, but if you just do little things consistently, you will see results, and those results will be positive results. If you did nothing more than put ten dollars a month away faithfully, it ends up being a lot of funds and providing a lot of income over time. It's just believing it, owning it, and deciding you can do it.

For parents that means avoiding telling your kids the old sayings we used to hear. Money doesn't grow on trees? Yes it does. Ask the owner of an orchard or lumber mill. You have to have a plan. Take control of the money. Pass that mindset on to your children. You control your money. You control your investments, and you need to make sure you're putting money aside for your investments. You dictate it. It's your life. You get to choose what you're doing.

If you start helping your kids understand this while they are teenagers, then they are going to be far ahead of most other people because the time value of money is exponential growth. It is a mathematical certainty that the more they put away when they're younger, the more likely they will be financially successful when they reach retirement.

Your beliefs are going to change your behaviors because now you know that you have control and you believe that if you do this, if you invest consistently and over a long period of time, you're going to get huge results and those results will absolutely happen as a result. That's all you have to do. Flip that switch.

Chapter 4
How to Calculate Your Income Spread

Frank remembers his "Oh shit!" moment very clearly. It happened on the night his wife threw him a fifty-fifth birthday party. Their tradition was to not follow the trend of having a bash on the "big" birthdays that ended in zero like everyone else did. Instead they would have a small celebration when they reached an age that ended in five—what they called in their family the "nickel" birthdays. The party was nothing over the top, just an enjoyable night with about twenty of their friends and family members. At the party several people, in separate conversations, asked Frank, "How much longer do you plan to work?" Later that night Frank couldn't sleep. He could not stop himself from ruminating about the "how much longer" question. He always just assumed he would work in his job as an executive at a software company until he couldn't. He liked his job well enough, but he started comparing himself with other people he knew that were his age who had already retired. All of them stayed busy, and they certainly seemed to have enough money somehow to more than meet their living expenses.

Unable to sleep, Frank got out of bed, sat down at the kitchen table with his laptop, and started trying to figure out when exactly he could retire. He thought he needed to figure out his net worth, but wasn't sure how to do that, so he created a spreadsheet with two columns. In the left column he listed revenue (his salary, his wife's salary, and income from a stock account he owned). What about their retirement accounts? Are those assets? Equity in their home? It was two-thirds paid for. Surely that counted. In the right-hand column, he listed their debt. To his surprise he couldn't say, exactly, how much money they owed. He listed credit card debt, their mortgage, and student loan balance remaining from when his wife decided on a midcareer job change and decided to get a master's degree.

The right-hand column was much longer than the left-hand one. Frank quickly realized that the reason retirement was nowhere in his future was that he needed to work to pay off their debt. Doing so felt like he was trying to cross a finish line that kept moving away from him.

So far in this book we have learned about financial imprisonment and what that really means. We've also learned about the number-one difference between the wealthy and the poor. Now it's time to do what Frank tried to do —start putting numbers to it. In this chapter you're going to learn how to calculate your income spread. In financial services there are three essential rules. Rule number one is calculate. Rule number two is a lot like number one: it's calculate. And then rule number three is, well, as you probably figured out, calculate.

WHAT I LEARNED FROM THE NUNS (AND THE IRS)

Tax comes from the Latin term *taxare*, which means to censure or express severe disapproval in something. I went to Catholic school, and we had nuns teaching some of the classes. The funny thing about nuns is that every now and then one of the nuns would express her severe disapproval with someone by issuing a whack (think ruler + hand or eraser + body). If someone was goofing off, they got a whack. On the other hand, if someone did something really good in class or did some helpful public service, they got a little pat on the head and some positive reinforcement in the form of nice comments.

Which would you rather have? The whack or the pat on the head?

The IRS is no different. It whacks certain types of income. For example, if you are out there working hard for wages at McDonald's, you learn very quickly that you have all these different taxes—FUTA, SUTA, old age, death, and survivors, Medicare, withholding for federal, withholding for state. It seems like everybody gets a cut of your money before you ever see it.

When I was growing up, I worked at McDonald's and made close to four dollars per hour at the time. If I worked forty hours, I assumed I would receive $160 on my check. Guess what? When I received my paycheck, it was far less because of tax withholding, workmen's compensation, Social Security taxes, and a variety of other fees and taxes I did not understand. I felt like I had just received a "whack" when I saw all of that money leave my paycheck. Chances are you are getting a bunch of whacks from the IRS.

By comparison, let's look at the rich. They sell some real estate for hundreds of thousands more than they paid for it and they don't even have to pay tax on it because they rolled it into more real estate. They sell that at a profit and buy even more and, you guessed it, no tax. When they pass away, not only is there no tax, but their heirs will receive massive tax write-offs. They don't get a whack; they get a pat on the head from the IRS.

The good news is that we can track the various types of income to see where the wealthiest Americans make money. And guess what? They're not over here getting whacked all the time on their income. In fact, only a small fraction of their income is getting whacked. The majority of their income is from the sources where they're getting the little pat on the head from the IRS.

It is up for you to decide: Do you want whacks on the knuckles or pats on the head? If it is pats on the head, keep reading because the types of investments we will be discussing are tax-favored and give you lots of pats. If you like the whacks, there is not much I can do for you, but the IRS sure loves you.

SOMETIMES YOUR BROKER MAKES YOU BROKER

Let me ask you a question. Two minus three equals five—is that true? No, of course not. It's false math. The problem is, your broker may be trying to use this math on you.

I had a client who was one of the early Microsoft employees. She had so much money that she had enough funds to cover herself and do philanthropy, and that's what she wanted to do for the rest of her life. One day she called me, sobbing, because her financial broker had "unretired her," as she put it. Suddenly her dream was shot, and she was just worrying about getting by. She didn't even have enough money coming in to cover her expenses, and it was because her broker convinced her that two minus three equals five and led her into some terrible investments.

You have to do your math. The numbers are our friends, but we have to be able to define them because brokers and others try to use secret language on us. They try to distract and confuse us. If somebody says an investment makes you money, it better be increasing your bank account. If your bank account is getting smaller, then two minus three equals negative one. Two minus three does not equal five, right? It's just doing your own math so you can detect when a broker is offering you a false conclusion.

DEFINING THE TERMS

In order to do this, we're going to have to get clarity on some very basic financial terms. Let's start with the word *income*. It's one of the financial terms that means exactly what it sounds like—money that comes in. Next is *expense*—money that goes out. I don't want to hear someone say, "I have income because I hold stocks that have increased in value." The problem with that concept is that you didn't sell anything. That's not income by our definition. It isn't paying you anything. It isn't putting money in your bank account—until you sell it.

An *asset* is something that produces income. But if you listen to a banker, they will say it's anything of value. They're going to tell you that your RV and your car and your house are assets. No, they're not. They're big fat liabilities. In the Infinity World, an asset is something that pays you. A liability is something that takes your money away. When we do the math, we can identify what a liability is. It's pulling money out of my account every month or every quarter or every year. It's not putting money in it. If your account did not grow, then it is not an asset. It's a liability. I don't care what the bankers and brokers call it.

Principal is the base. If I have $100,000 that I invest in something, that's my principal. If I borrow money or loan money, the principal is the value of that original loan. The *interest* is what you pay on it for the privilege of borrowing. Or, conversely, what you're getting paid for loaning it—which gets you a pat on the head. Furthermore, you might not have to pay certain types of taxes on it. Another pat on the head. That means that you want to be the one earning the interest. You don't want to be paying interest to somebody else and getting the whack.

There are two kinds of interest we need to be aware of. *Simple interest* means that you pay a set amount every year on the principal. If you borrow $100,000 at 4 percent, you pay $4,000 per year. If you don't make a payment on the $104,000, then the next year you owe $108,000. Instead of paying 4 percent on the $104,000, you pay 4 percent on just the principal. That's how simple interest works. The same rule applies if you are earning simple interest on an investment. You are paid a set amount every year based on the principal. If you invest $100,000 at 4 percent, you make $4,000 in interest each year.

One of the reasons investors get wealthy is due to *compound interest*. If your $100,000 investment is paying you compound interest, that means that you are making interest on the principal and the interest earned. If you invest $100,000 at 4 percent compounded annually, you make $4,000 in interest the first year. But the second year, you earn interest on $104,000 and would receive $4,160. That doesn't seem like a big difference, but over time it snowballs dramatically.

Let's compare the difference between simple and compound interest. In both cases you invest $100,000. At the end of twenty-five years of collecting simple interest, your investment is worth twice as much as the initial investment, or $200,000. Not bad. If you invest the same amount at the same interest rate but compounding, your initial investment will be worth $266,584 at the end of twenty-five years.

Compound interest can also work against you. If you have credit card debt, you are paying compound interest on your monthly balance. According to the Federal Reserve's data for the fourth quarter of 2019, the average credit card interest rate was 14.87 percent. In fact, the rates for 2019 were the highest recorded since 1995.[5] And that is just the average rate. The interest rate at the high end is upward of 25 percent. You can see how these interest rates, compounding on unpaid balances, can quickly become a crisis for people. One of the leading killers of marriages is financial struggles, and the cause of financial struggles is often credit card debt. The compound interest just kept growing, and you feel like you can never pay it off. You would think people would pay attention to this huge pothole in the road and avoid credit card debt, but that isn't the case. The *Wall Street Journal* reported that credit card debt reached a record at the end of 2019.[6] The number of people who are seriously behind on their credit card payments increased as well—particularly among younger credit card users.

Albert Einstein allegedly said, "Compound interest is the eighth wonder of the world. He who understands it, earns it; he who doesn't, pays it." You can see that you want to avoid paying compound interest and find ways to earn it. And how do you do that? You have investments that continue to compound. And they keep growing on that value and based on what happens in the economy. When you look at a dividend-producing stock, that dividend should be growing every year. That's money that continues to get bigger and bigger. It's compounding every year, so that thirty years from now, a company that you paid a small amount for with a 3 percent or 4 percent dividend, compared to the original price, is paying back 100 percent a year.

Because your money is compounding annually, it is growing exponentially over time. In the first few years, it may not be great, but the longer it sits, the bigger it gets, and it just starts growing like crazy. Because if you are paying something, it's snowballing against you. But if you're getting paid, it's snowballing in your benefit. You do not want to be paying compound interest, but you absolutely do want to be earning it.

Your *net* is the difference between income and an expense. Let's say you're making $10,000 a month and you're spending $7,000. Your net is $10,000 minus $7,000, or $3,000. Your net income is what you have left.

In order to better understand income and expense statements, let's go into a bit more detail, first on income. According to the IRS, there are eight types of income.

- *Wages*: This is the money that you are earning.
- *Profits*: What you are making off of a business.
- *Rents*: What you're getting paid for someone else's use of an asset, like renting a house.
- *Royalties*: Typically this is money earned from intellectual property. To

be honest, very few of you are going to have royalty income unless you write a book, music, or software.

- *Dividends*: These are the payments from *capital-C corporations* where they pay you a part of their profits. In the United States we actually pay about half as much tax on dividends as we pay on other income.

- *Interest*: This is money that you make off of principal. If you loan somebody money and you're getting paid back the principal plus an agreed-upon amount each month, you made a little bit of interest income.

- *Short-term capital gains*: This is where you sell something of value. Real estate is a great example. If you buy a house and sell the house within a year, that's short-term capital gains.

- *Long-term capital gains*: If you hold that same house for more than a year, then you have long-term capital gains.

NOT ALL SOURCES ARE TREATED THE SAME

The IRS doesn't view all of these income sources the same way. This is a critical factor for building your Infinity Income. In our system these three income sources fall into three buckets.

Bad Bucket: Wages get the biggest whack from the IRS. If you work at McDonald's and you're making $30,000 a year, whack, whack, whack, whack. You get hit with old age, survivors, and disability insurance at 14.1 percent. McDonald's pays half; you pay half. For Medicare, McDonald's pays half, you pay half, 2.9 percent. You pay all of some of these as well: federal unemployment, state unemployment, workmen's comp, plus labor and industries. All of these are getting drawn out of your wages before anyone hands you a check. You also pay federal income tax withholding, and you pay state income tax withholding if your state has income taxes. This means that in a week when you make $400, you might get to keep $330, and probably less.

The other giant whack from the IRS perspective is self-employment income. If you're working for yourself as a sole proprietor, the whacks start. First, you're going to get audited more. Second, you're not going to get all the write-offs you're entitled to. Third, you can't do an accountable plan because you are a tax disadvantage from a tax standpoint. And fourth, every dollar that you make is subject to self-employment taxes. It's a complete whack-a-thon.

Better Bucket: By comparison, rents, royalties, and interest are okay. With these, you don't pay any Social Security taxes or Medicare. Royalties, interest, and short-term capital gains are taxed at your ordinary bracket, though. So while they're okay, they're not great. You're still paying on them at your tax bracket. You avoided a big chunk of tax, but you still have some tax, and it's not the greatest tax rate. So what is the best income from a tax perspective?

Infinity Bucket: The best income source is real estate. I may never pay tax on real estate, and neither will my family. I could own real estate and it could grow from a dollar to $10 million, and I will have paid nothing in tax. Zero. Meanwhile, the guy at McDonald's made $400 and paid more in taxes than I did, and I made 10 million bucks. That's real estate. The IRS is telling you what to invest in.

What about dividends? They're taxed at long-term capital gain rates at either 0 percent, 15 percent, or 20 percent, depending on what your tax bracket is.

If you're in the highest tax bracket, which federally is 37 percent, your highest federal income tax bracket for dividends is 20 percent. If you're in the lowest tax bracket at zero, your dividends are taxed at zero. Long term sale of capital assets is taxed the same way.

Your maximum federal income tax treatment on that long-term sale is 20 percent on the capital gains. If you as an individual tax payer make that same money but it isn't long-term capital gains, you're starting at 37 percent, plus paying old age, survivors, and disability, as well as Medicare and any other applicable state taxes, unemployment taxes, labor and industry, and perhaps others. All those things whack you if you're making wages versus selling a capital asset. Selling a capital asset only gives you half of the tax whack, and sometimes less than half.

EVERYTHING YOU NEED TO KNOW ABOUT HOLDING ASSETS YOU CAN LEARN FROM PLAYING MONOPOLY

My holding period is forever. I don't want to sell assets. Have you ever played Monopoly? When you first start playing, what do you do every time you land on a square that somebody hasn't already bought something on? You buy whatever they're selling. You're accumulating assets. What if you just sold it the next round to another player for cash? You would lose. You win by not selling for cash. You win by continuing to grow your asset base. You may sell something strategically to invest in something else so you can expand and make another property even better, like building a hotel.

But you are not building Infinity wealth by selling your long-term capital assets and turning them into cash. Cash is not an asset unless is it earning a return, which it might not be doing if it is sitting in your checking account. There is also the problem of inflation, but we will hold off on that for now. As soon as you sell the asset for cash, you no longer own that asset or its cash flow. Remember, you are in the business of accumulating assets that pay you money. That is the Infinity Bucket. The other buckets? I call them "carrying buckets," from a fable about finances I read. I believe it was written by a financial planner—but it makes the point in a very powerful way.

Once upon a time, long, long ago, two men named Bruno and Pablo lived in a tiny Italian village that needed water. There was a cistern in the middle of the town, and the villagers all chipped in to pay to keep it filled with water. The mayor of the town asked for proposals from locals to keep the cistern full by carrying water from a spring about two miles away. Bruno and Pablo submitted proposals, and both won the job at one coin per bucket of water (which was a lot of money back in those days).

They started toting buckets from the spring to the cistern and determined that they could do about twenty buckets a day. It was very hard work carrying those heavy buckets full of water, but they made a lot of money. In fact, by local standards, they got rich.

One day Bruno told Pablo, "I'm going to live it up. I'm going to go out and eat and drink and have a good time." They didn't have cars back then, so he bought a fancy donkey and used it to impress his friends. Pablo approached Bruno one day and said, "Why don't we dig a trench? We can put a pipe in it, and that will bring all the water we will ever need to the cistern. Plus, we won't have to carry all these buckets."

And Bruno said, "No way. We have a good thing going, and I'm making a ton of money. Why upset the apple cart?" They continued carrying buckets. But Pablo used his money to buy little pieces of land from the farmers between the spring and the cistern. Then, every night when he finished carrying buckets, Pablo would go out into the countryside and dig his trench. He kept digging, slowly but steadily. After a year he was about halfway there, and he installed a pipeline that reached to the halfway point. All of a sudden, he didn't have to walk as far to carry his buckets. He was able to cut back the amount of time it took him to carry buckets, and he could double his productivity.

Eventually Pablo completed the pipeline all the way to the cistern. What happened to Bruno's money? The village no longer needed Bruno to carry buckets. The water flowed right to the cistern, and Pablo owned the pipeline. Pablo had a dependable source of income that didn't involve carrying buckets.

Now what if he sold the pipeline? Well, he would have a lump of one-time money. Pablo was very clear that he didn't want to sell the pipeline. He had invested his time and labor digging it, and now the water just kept flowing in, and so did his income. If you build a pipeline, guess what you don't have to do anymore? You don't have to carry buckets.

Now you might say, "I love carrying buckets. It keeps me in shape, gets me outside, and the villagers appreciate me." How does this translate for you to your real job? Maybe you like teaching or doing whatever job you have. I get that. I like my job. I love teaching, so I'll always be doing it even though I have tons of Infinity Income coming in. It allows me to do whatever I want to do.

WHAT DO THE WEALTHY DO?

Now let's look at the wealthy and try to figure out what they do. A great place to start is to look at the data that the IRS publishes every year in something called the IRS Data Book, which anyone can access.[7] It tells us that for people who make over a million dollars a year, 36 percent of their income comes from the Infinity Bucket—17 percent from capital gain and 47 percent from rents, royalties, dividends, and interest. These are the profits that come off of passive investments.

What are the rich not doing? Selling income-generating assets. That's a minority of their income. Where do they make most of their money? Right there in that asset category. This is Infinity Income. Just over a third is coming from work. They still do it, but that's not where they're making most of their money. They're making most of their money from their Infinity Bucket. They may still earn wages, but there is often a specific reason for it. They want to qualify for certain lending, or maybe they're putting it into a tax deferred plan. There are lots of reason some people still want to have wage income. Sometimes they just have to because they own businesses that they are required to take a salary from, depending on how it's set up. But it's the minority of their income. All of this goes back to the idea of mindset. Once you believe this is possible for you, you understand how it works, and you see the data, it's hard to argue against its effectiveness.

Let's look at some additional statistics. For people with an annual income exceeding $1 million:

- 65 percent of them have at least three sources of income.

- 45 percent have income from four sources.

- 29 percent have income from more than five.

Think about this: two-thirds of rich people have at least three of these income sources. Do you want to be rich? I suggest you need to have at least three sources of income. Start building those up. Rents, royalties, dividends, interest, capital gains, both short term and long term, all come from assets, not from you working. In other words, you're not trading your hours for money. The asset makes the money. Those types of income sources don't require you. You don't have to carry buckets for them because it's pipeline money. You could always have a job, but you would be working because you like to. You may not be able to help it. Because you're so good at whatever you're doing, you may just end up becoming a consultant.

One of my favorite stories is from Brian Tracy, who tells a great story about a consultant. It seems there was an energy plant that was having serious problems that the plant engineers could not resolve. This consultant was a troubleshooter who was well-known in the industry as the guy that fixes the kind of problem they were facing. When they approached him, the consultant said, "Ten thousand bucks. I'll be there tomorrow."

He showed up, walked into one room, and spent a while looking at a series of monitors and readouts. He made one test and said, "Change that fuse right there, and your problem's fixed." Then he left. He was there for all of thirty minutes. When he sent his invoice for $10,000, the plant manager said, "That's excessive. You were only here for a half an hour. Why am I going to pay you ten thousand dollars for a half an hour?" The consultant said, "That's fine. Don't pay me anything for my time." Then he revised his invoice to read, "Time, zero. Knowing where the problem was, $10,000." The moral of the story is that he had very specific knowledge. Sometimes you get paid a bunch of money just because you have specified knowledge. That's going to be part of that 36 percent of income. It's not McDonald's hourly wage money. It's knowing how to be a consultant to McDonald's and have them pay you a bunch for what you know.

CALCULATE FOR INFINITY

To make it easier for you to do the calculations for yourself, we have developed something called the Infinity Calculator. It will do all the math for you after you plug in the income sources for you or you and your spouse/partner. You can find the calculator on our website at: andersonadvisors.com/infinity-calculator/.

If you are not using the calculator right now, let me explain the basic approach we use to calculate for Infinity.

Total Monthly Income: First, you add up your total income sources. If you have a spouse/partner, you do add in their income amounts as well. The total income should include all sources included in the list below, plus any other income sources you have.

- Wages
- Tips
- Commissions
- Bonuses
- Interest
- Dividends
- Net profits from businesses
- Net profits from rental properties
- Income from alimony
- IRA income
- Pension payments
- Veteran's benefits
- Unemployment benefits
- Royalties
- Other income

Total monthly income $_____

There are a few things to consider when compiling your total income list. If you have a business that flows onto your return, include that information as well. Also include net profits from rental profits. Why do I say net profit from rental profits? It's because we care about what actually hits your account. If you have incoming rent of $1,000 per month, but you have a property manager taking 10 percent of it, plus you have some repairs and other miscellaneous charges, you're only netting $500. Remember that we are calculating this by the month. If you get something quarterly, divide it by three. If you get something annually, divide it by twelve.

Total Monthly Expenses: Earlier in the book we discussed wants compared to needs. For now we are going to look at our expenses as our wants. When calculating expenses, many people tend to overlook some of the things they spend money on. Remember that the more accurate you can be, the better. Don't forget to include everything, no matter how small it seems.

- Rent payment

- Mortgage

- Utilities

- Homeowner's or renter's insurance

- Household repairs

- Property taxes

- Cable/internet

- Streaming TV services

- Mobile phone

- Auto payments

- Auto insurance

- Gas

- Train, bus, rideshare, and other transportation

- Groceries/food

- Credit card payments

- Installment contract payments

- Alimony

- Child support

- Childcare

- Charity/religious institutions

- Medical expenses

- Dental expenses

- Prescriptions

- Life insurance

- Long-term care insurance

- Personal maintenance

- Recreation/entertainment

- Gym membership

- Hobby expenses

- Vacation/travel

- Dry cleaning/laundry

- Holiday/birthday gifts

- Other expenses

Total monthly expenses $_____

The calculator will help you to figure out what your fat is. What can you cut out that isn't a need? Could you cut out your cable bill? Could you cut out going to the movies or clubs? I understand that you may not want to cut these expenses. But could you do without them if you had to in a pinch? Are they ongoing expenses that you don't really need? Are some of them services you forgot you are paying for? Look back at your list of expenses, and put an asterisk next to the ones that might be fat. You could now subtract the fat from your monthly expense total. Your wants minus your fat equals your need.

The reason this is important is that it's going to show you what we could do if you wanted to. If you're willing to live off of what you need instead of what you want for a while, you may be able to quickly change the amount of your money available for Infinity Investing and end up living a life long-term that you didn't think was possible. But for now we're just doing an income statement, so subtract your expenses from your income.

Total monthly income $_____

– Total monthly expenses $_____

= Income spread $_____

Income Spread: I'll use an example of the Joneses, who are making $7,500 per month. Their want is $6,500, so their net income is $1,000. $7,500 minus $6,500 is $1,000. That is their *income spread*. When the Joneses reviewed and modified their wants list, they realized they could, relatively painlessly, trim an additional $1,000 of fat from their monthly expenses. By doing so, the Joneses doubled their income spread to $2,000.

Go ahead and put pencil to paper now to calculate your income spread. It is critical to spend the time at this stage to calculate a number for yourself in order to set a goal. It's like trying to lose weight. You need to understand your current weight and the weight you want to achieve. You have to set goals that are quantifiable. Hopefully it's a positive number. If it's a negative number, then you have some work to do. If it's a positive number, it's immediately breathing some hope for you.

You start your Infinity Plan with any amount. Even if it is ten dollars, start to build the discipline of regular contributions. Replace the fat in your spread by investing that amount instead of spending it. We have a mastermind group that has a number of young people in their early twenties that are in Infinity. They have more money coming in from passive investments than they spend. There are two ways to do that. You either increase the amount of income that's coming in from those investments, or you reduce your expenses, or a combination of the two. One young man and his wife in the group live very frugally so they didn't have too far to go. But they still committed to a number, and it immediately allowed them to make an investment that they wouldn't have otherwise done.

They disregarded what the media or other people said about possible "better" investments available to them. Their position was "By doing this, we no longer have to work. We are now volunteering for working. By doing this, it enables us to not have to worry about our needs ever again. We have enough money coming in that we know that we have a roof over our head and food, shelter, and the basic necessities of life." Their mindset was that they had control of their money and they weren't going to be misled by somebody who wasn't a fiduciary. They recognized a good deal for them because it made sense based off of their carefully calculated income spread. They did it, and you can too.

Chapter 5

The Old Way of Calculating Net Worth (And Why We Should Dump It)

N ancy usually just glanced at the statements sent by her bank and brokerages. She admitted to herself that in the past, when she received these statements as hard copy in the mail, she spent more time with them. She also had less money back in those days and was being more attentive to every dollar. Nowadays she would receive an email, one of seemingly one hundred per day, informing her that she could log on to her account and review her statement, and it seemed like a hassle. She never really looked at what the statements said—only what the numbers at the top of the statements were—and she had grown accustomed to looking only at the summary of the data, like how much was in the account and how they said she was doing on her investments.

She surprised herself one January morning by making a pot of coffee and logging in to all of her accounts and spending a few hours reviewing and scrutinizing the details. She checked her bank accounts, her brokerage account, her retirement account, and a 529 plan set up for her children.

The previous year had been a good one for the economy of the country. The S&P had shot up, as had the value of most of her holdings. But she noticed something odd. Each account presented a summary of its growth over the past year expressed as a percentage. But when Nancy used her calculator to do the math herself, she discovered something troubling. The amount of money in her account was less than the claimed gain in the statement. In some of her accounts, it was close, but in her brokerage account especially, the dollar amount was substantially less than the purported percentage. Nancy was confused and concerned. Was there a mistake? Where was her money going? Why was it so confusing?

HOME IS WHERE THE HEART IS (IT'S ALSO WHERE OUR MONEY IS)

In this chapter you're going to learn about the old way of calculating your net income and why we need to toss it out. I call it the old way of calculating net worth because it is outdated and inaccurate. In order to understand this, we're going to have to take a deeper dive into net worth. In chapter 4 we reviewed income and expense statements, and now we're going to be focusing on the other side of the balance sheet, where we place assets and liabilities. We will review what your bank thinks your assets and liabilities are and why they're often wrong. We will learn how this fiction imprisons people, and this will likely lead to an "aha!" moment for you. If I asked you to name your biggest asset, what would you say? Nine out of ten people say it is their home. I also hear things like gold, their IRA, their cars or RV, or their 1952 Mickey Mantle baseball card. This is also how the banks think, and they sell you on this idea of what an asset is when you're doing your balance sheet. The problem is, not only are these things not assets, but they could in fact be disguised liabilities. We will discuss that soon.

But first let's use the old way to understand it better. It's going to help us come up with some numbers and nail things down. Make a list of everything you consider an asset. Don't forget to include things like:

• Checking account balance

- Savings account

- Stocks (non-IRA or 401(k))

- Bonds

- Vested pension

- 401(k)

- Accounts receivable

- Cash value of life insurance

- Tax refund due

- Boat

- Recreational vehicle

- Vacation home

- Autos

- House

- Rental real estate

- IRA

- Home furnishings

- Collectibles

- Tools

- Other assets

Total assets $_____

Whatever it is, whatever it's worth, if you could sell it and get your hands on the cash, you're going to be listing it here. And again, you can use our online Infinity Calculator to do this. If you have an income statement that you completed in the last year or so, use it as a starting point. You could also use a recent mortgage application as a starting point.

On the flip side, if you owe something to someone else, you're going to list those liabilities. On this list you would include things like:

- Mortgage on personal home
- Mortgage on rental properties
- Mortgage on vacation home
- Auto loans
- Recreational vehicle loan
- Boat loan
- Medical bills
- Dental bills
- Credit card balances
- Other revolving credit
- Contingent liabilities
- Taxes payable
- Judgment payable
- College loans
- Money owed to individuals
- Contracts payable
- Other liabilities

Total liabilities $_____

Don't forget to include liabilities from signing off on something for a child or cosigning for somebody else. If you are doing this with your spouse or partner, include all obligations for both people. We're going to add all these things up to calculate your total liabilities. This is going to give you your net worth. Your total assets minus your total liabilities equals your net worth. For example, let's just say your assets totaled up to $500,000, and your liabilities were $200,000. Using this old method, your net worth is $300,000.

Total assts $_____

– Total liabilities $_____

= Net worth $_____

THE PROBLEM WITH THIS APPROACH

This approach is dead wrong, and it comes down to something very simple. You could have a big house worth a million bucks. It has a mortgage of $500,000, so you figure you have $500,000 in net worth. But do you really? The next day you lose your job. Are you going to be able to get a loan on the remaining equity? No, because you no longer have a job and your house is a pretend asset. You lost your job, but you still have to pay the mortgage, utilities, homeowner's insurance, and property taxes on it. All of a sudden this house you thought was your main asset is a big, fat, huge liability, and you're stuck with it. I see clients get into financial trouble over and over again because somebody told them their biggest asset was their home, and they figured the biggest home they could buy would create the biggest asset. But as the old saying goes, if you're starving, you can't eat your house.

Cars, like houses, are also liabilities. An asset puts money in your account. You could take that money and you could exchange it for groceries. That's an asset. If you can eat it, if it can feed you, it's an asset. Liabilities starve you. They take the money out of your pocket. They destroy you. I have seen many families and many businesses get overwhelmed by those liabilities. They have a house that they couldn't afford and expenses that they couldn't pay for. It slowly bled them to death until they were in bankruptcy or foreclosure. That false asset mindset puts good people into bad situations. Your house is not your biggest asset. It is a liability. Then you add another liability on top of it by getting a mortgage. All of a sudden, you are working for the bank or mortgage company. That's a classic example of financial imprisonment. Now you are working your butt off to pay for something that somebody else owns. The asset is that actual mortgage. Unfortunately, it is the bank's asset, not yours.

We have a very simple rule about liabilities. You want to make sure that you have an asset-producing income to cover the liabilities. Remember that in my story about when I moved to Las Vegas, I had my liabilities covered by assets. I had those rents coming in. I could live off them. I could eat groceries from them because they were true assets. My liability was the house we rented to live in, but I didn't have to worry about any fluctuations in its value because I didn't own it. I didn't pretend like it was an asset.

Is your car an asset or a liability? Does it feed you? If you have a Rolls-Royce, is that bringing you money? If you own it, it's just costing you money, and that is a clear liability. And then you probably took out a loan to buy it, which is also a liability. Like many Americans, you're buying a liability with a liability, and that's always a bad idea.

Credit cards are probably the worst. You end up working for the credit card company because compound interest accumulates so fast, and the way it is set up, you pay the interest first. It works the same way with a mortgage. You are paying the interest first instead of paying down the principal on the debt. If you have a high credit card balance, and you just pay the minimum, you're more than thirty years away from paying it off. That is imprisonment. You are working for the credit card company now. Sorry to have to be the person that tells you that, but you are literally putting yourself in a situation where you're supporting them by your hard work.

Now let me be clear. I'm not telling you that homeownership is bad. What I'm saying is you don't buy a liability with a liability. I'll show you how to own your house, but you're not going to own it so that it's somebody else's asset and we're just paying them.

IS THE COST OF COLLEGE STILL WORTH IT?

Maybe you are in a situation where you can't become a homeowner because you're carrying too much student loan debt. Maybe you got a degree because somebody told you that this was going to be a very valuable degree. For the most part, there is some value to getting a degree. But it's not guaranteed, and it doesn't work the same way for every field. A college degree, on average, is going to increase your earnings over a lifetime about a million dollars, so is the expense worth it today? Is it worth the $200,000 to $300,000 that some schools can set you back? If you invest $100,000, you should have around a million bucks after thirty years. If you pay $100,000 for your degree, it's probably worth it in the long term. If you pay $200,000 and all you're going to do is increase your salary by a million dollars over your lifetime, then maybe it's not such a good idea. (But remember that million-dollar figure is the average.)

We know that doctors, engineers, and lawyers are skewing that average. If I'm an English major who graduates making $40,000 a year, then I subsidized the education of the engineer who's making $400,000. How? Because the degree cost us both the same price. Again, we've brainwashed our kids into thinking that all degrees are of equal value. They're not. You don't want to go $200,000 in debt for that English degree. I'm sorry, it's just not a good decision. That is a liability. You're going to be working to pay off that student loan for the rest of your life. Take it from me. In my work I look at people's balance sheets every day, and I see the impact of these decisions. I have numerous clients that are decades out of their institutions, and they've yet to really make a dent in the principal balances on those student debts. They cannot get rid of it. That is not a cliché because student debt is almost impossible to discharge in bankruptcy. It will follow you around the rest of your life if you are not careful.

YOUR MONEY, YOUR RISK, THEIR GAIN

There are other examples of financial imprisonment. I showed you what it looks like when you have a broker who is churning your account, using your money to pay themselves. You are taking 100 percent of the risk with your investments. They are taking, on average, about 70 percent of the benefit. I'm just giving you the average. Some take way more. And if you lose your money in the market, they don't pay for it. They got paid to lose your money. They might mean well, and I'm sure they don't try to cause you to lose your money. But if they do, there's no negative ramification for them other than they might lose a client—if the client is paying attention. But for you, you're out all your money.

Let's use a simple example. If you have an account with $100,000 in it and you lose 20 percent in the market that year, what do you have left? You have $80,000. Now the next year, it goes up 20 percent. Wall Street would tell you that you're even. Let's do the math. Twenty percent of $80,000 is $16,000. Your gain would be $16,000, so you'd be at $96,000. Your net is still −4 percent. You're $4,000 in the hole because you're down to $96,000. You started with $100,000, so you are less than breaking even. That's called being a financial prisoner to somebody else so that they can prosper off of your assets.

Following the crowd is tempting, but it's usually not a good idea. Before the burst of the real estate bubble, everyone was saying, "Hey, this is a great market. Any real estate in New York, California, Las Vegas—it's only going to go up in value." In Las Vegas people were buying a $500,000 house that they could rent for only $2,500 and the mortgage on that darn thing was $3,500. They were losing money every month. But some real estate agent suckered them into buying it, saying it's a great market. It's going to go up from $500,000. It's going to be an asset. It's going to be worth $800,000.

I've got news for you: until you sell it, it is a liability. There are transactional costs to selling your house that will eat up about 8 to 10 percent of the sale price. If I have a $500,000 house, it's really a $450,000 house, and that's if I could sell it right away and somebody gave me full price. It's not an asset.

Rental property is only an asset if it's feeding you, putting more money in your pocket than it's taking out. If it's taking out more money than it's putting in, it's a liability. Don't let anybody tell you differently. Do the numbers yourself. Add it all up. A real simple rule of thumb is that if you have a rental property, expect that 50 percent of the rents are going to make it into your account. If f you have a property renting at $2,500 a month, you're going to see $1,250 of it. Don't forget that you've got to pay the debt on it. You have real estate taxes and everything that goes along with home ownership on that rental. You're going to have to pay a property manager, or you will have to manage it. You're going to have to paint it. You're going to have to replace roofs, HVACs, all other systems. These are all costs you have to factor in. And then if it's positive, it's an asset; if it's negative, it's a liability.

When I work with clients who are in financial turmoil, they tell me it feels like they are suffocating, or choking, like somebody has their hand right on their throat. They say it feels like drowning and they can't keep their head above water. These are not pretty adjectives. Oppressed, destroyed, distraught, depressed, no hope. This is what financial imprisonment feels like.

In the next chapters, I am going to describe specific action items that you can start on right now to prevent or get you out of financial imprisonment. It reminds me of some mountain climbing trips I've taken where you just keep moving forward to get to the top. I've even climbed a glacier, and I remember it seemed like we were just plodding along: "Chunk, chunk, chunk." You're at a high elevation, you can barely breathe, and your instructions are to just keep moving up. Eventually you'll reach the peak. You don't have to sprint up the glacier. You don't have to run up the mountain. Once at a conference I heard a speaker who made a big impression on me. He talked about his experience summiting Mount Everest. And the thing that made his feat all the more impressive is that he is blind. He described taking one step a minute toward the top because they had so little oxygen. On top of that, since he couldn't see, he was following the sound of a bell. He said the winds were so high that they were clinging onto their ice axes. As long as you're moving in the right direction, you will reach the summit at some point. And from this point forward, we're heading toward that summit. You just keep going one step at a time and you'll get to the top. And let me tell you, the view from the top is terrific.

What should you take away from this chapter?

- How net worth has been traditionally calculated, and why we should dump it.

- Should you count your house as an asset? What about your car?

- Why credit card debt is so dangerous.

- Is your college degree an asset, and is it worth the cost?

Chapter 6
How to Convert Your Old Numbers into Infinity Numbers

Walton was an older real estate agent who ran a small business. Like many real estate agents, Walton liked to teach new agents the ropes and enjoyed the process of making deals. What really set Walton's office apart from other real estate businesses was his requirement that his staff invest in the product that they were selling—residential real estate.

Walton told his staff to take at least 10 percent of their income and make sure that they were investing in real estate. More specifically, he wanted them investing in rental properties for the community, and he *required* this if you wanted to work for him. The type of properties he invested in were called cash-flow properties, meaning they brought in more rents than it cost the agent to own the property. If a property rented for $1,000 per month, the agent needed to be able to pay expenses, repairs, insurance, taxes, and any mortgage payments and still have money left over. The agents seemed to like the idea, and Walton never had to do much to convince them to buy. They had a constant flow of deals coming through the office, and Walton always helped them calculate the good buys.

One of the younger agents was confused about the requirement for buying investment real estate instead of just buying a bigger home for himself. The young agent's parents had always taught him that his home was his best investment. As a result, he thought that a bigger and more expensive home must be the way to go—after all, it was his biggest investment. The young agent had been raised to believe that you bought a house and, because the value would increase, you could sell it, make money, and buy an even bigger house. Walton, however, only talked about purchasing. He never talked about selling, and he talked about holding real estate in your asset portfolio.

But what about selling it when the market went up? The young agent was flummoxed and did not understand why Walton was focused more on the rents from a property than the property value itself. In fact, Walton would often laugh and joke about the value of his own real estate portfolio, saying, "I don't know and don't wanna know—I am not selling." The young agent thought to himself that the portfolio must be worth a fortune and if it were his, he would sell it and buy the biggest house in the best neighborhood and really enjoy life.

But Walton kept on doing what he was doing. He would train the people in his office and get them prepared to pass their licensing exam so that they could become real estate agents. But his requirement was always the same— that they set aside at least 10 percent of their hard-earned money and invest it into real estate assets. Ten percent seemed like a lot of money at the time, but it really was not that bad.

As the years went on and the investments his people had grew, something amazing started happening. The agents grew happier because they were able to take more time off. They were less stressed because they had additional income streams from the properties they owned. They also shared what they did with their clients, and the clients would invest as well. The young agent had friends outside of work and would sometimes share what he was doing with his friends since they all seemed to be pretty stressed about money. He told them what he did and how he always invested at least 10 percent of his income, that it was easy and that he often invested more. His friends would laugh and would respond that they could barely get by now with their mortgages, car payments, school loans, and various other expenses.

Over the years the young agent built up quite a portfolio of real estate. In fact, the agent was investing almost 100 percent of his money into deals because he could live off the income from the first properties he bought. That was about the time the agent realized what Walton was actually teaching him when he first started as a young agent those many years before.

WAKE-UP CALL

In this chapter you will learn how to convert your old numbers from chapter 4 into new Infinity calculations and how to then use that information. We already discussed the old ways banks think about our numbers and how that is a disadvantage to us. Those old numbers are not completely useless, but we have to convert them. It's useful data if you know what to do with it. We are going to take that data and learn which parts of it count as Infinity Income sources and learn how to reverse engineer your numbers so you know exactly what your Infinity net worth is. Your Infinity net worth, in a nutshell, is how many days you could live without working. It will show you how many days you can live without picking up buckets and carrying water to the village cistern.

Remember that effective Infinity Investing means calculating the amount of income you need to live. You need to consider your passive sources of income. That will tell you how much income you need to live by knowing what your wants and needs are. Then you just have to figure out where the assets are that are going to produce it. Here's a quiz. You will have to use your mind's eye for this one. Picture a typical farm. What are the assets? Is it the silo? Is it that tractor? Is it the rooster that's on the tractor? Is it the farmhouse? What are the assets on the farm?

Let's conduct an analysis. Is the tractor an asset? Does the tractor feed me? Does the farmhouse feed me? Do the silos feed me? You know what feeds me? It's none of that. It's the crops. The fields are assets. It's the corn, the wheat, the soybeans—whatever I'm growing I should count as assets. This is tricky because I don't necessarily need all of the farm equipment to have this farm feed me.

Heck, I could own it and I could have somebody else sharecrop it. If I do that, someone else farms the land and they pay me part of the profit. They grow all the crops, and they pay me. I don't have to lift a finger. With the reduction of family farms, this arrangement is happening all over the country. Or I can do it myself, but I know that the asset has to exceed the cost of running the farm. That farmhouse and all of the equipment come at a price. I'm just storing the crops in the silos, which is a metaphor for my 401(k), my IRA, or my defined benefit plan. I have to protect it by paying attention to it. I have to make sure that I don't have rats in my silo eating all of my crops. The rats are the brokers. They'll eat it up if I'm not careful, so I have to keep a close eye on it. If you're a broker, I apologize. You may be a goodhearted broker, but unfortunately, I'm an attorney, so I'm just going to tell you, there are brokers out there that give the industry a bad name.

You will remember from chapter 1 how important it is to use a fiduciary. A fiduciary is required to put your interests ahead of their own, and they won't create churn in your account to increase their commissions. They tend to be paid to manage a total portfolio of assets, and they're usually charging about 1 percent. That's who you should use to make sure that you are growing the crops best suited to your climate, and they protect them because that is their duty.

For some financial advisors, it's so much easier just to be a broker (rather than a fiduciary) because they can make clients "broker" and still get paid. If you're a fiduciary and you make your client broker, you're probably going to get sued because you owe them a duty, which is what happened in the Morgan Stanley example from the beginning of the book.

CALCULATED DECISIONS

There are a multitude of decisions that go into using your assets wisely. Some are common sense, and some might be counterintuitive. I address some of the most common life scenarios below. Should I lease or buy a car? Should I invest in an IRA? What about that 0 percent credit card? Should I put money in the stock market? How about rental properties? Remember that it all comes down to this—the three rules of anything financial are calculate, calculate, and calculate.

Buy or Lease a Car?

Which is better for you, to lease or buy a car? You need to calculate the cost of ownership and really crunch the numbers. I can tell you that in less than twenty years, you're probably never going to buy a traditional gas engine ever again. You're going to start buying electric or hybrid cars because the cost of ownership is so much lower. You have to figure out your total cost for any vehicle because you might buy a vehicle that you have to dump money into for repairs or end up with a gas hog. You have to add all that up to determine the true cost of car ownership compared to leasing.

Let's remember that the IRS give us a mileage reimbursement figure every year, and historically this has been between fifty-three and fifty-eight cents per mile. Depending on the price of gas and how much wear and tear you put on a vehicle, this will tell you about what it costs to maintain a vehicle. So if you're driving ten thousand miles a year, and the IRS mileage value is fifty-eight cents per mile, that's $5,800. Is leasing the car better under that scenario, or is buying the car better? You have to compare the two because the car is still a liability. Quite often people are better off leasing the car they want versus buying a car they want but way better off buying the car they *need*. The best answer is to buy an asset and budget your car purchase or lease based on the amount of money the asset produces on a monthly basis. For example, if I was able to buy a rental property that consistently yielded me $450 per month in positive cash flow, I might lease the car I wanted at something close to $450 per month.

Buy or Rent a House?

What about buying a house versus renting a house? Which is better? Well, it depends. If you can rent the house in the neighborhood where you want to live for half the price of what it would cost to buy it, you should rent it. You're going to calculate what it costs to live. There's a dollar figure that represents what it would cost for you to have shelter over your head, depending on whether it's a want or need. Could you go rent a four-hundred-square-foot apartment? You probably did that when you were starting out. Would you want to do that now? Probably not. But if you needed to, you could. You calculate what that number is. What's your want? This is where you want to live. Great; should you buy the house? It's still a liability no matter what, so you calculate the cost of ownership. Is the cost of ownership better than renting? Just compare it.

According to the Saint Louis Federal Reserve bank economic data (FRED), the cost of renting and buying the same home are virtually identical.[8] Unfortunately, when we buy a home, we often spend more because real estate agents are really good at telling us "how much house we can afford" instead of focusing on what we need and want. The 2008 great recession was based primarily on this mindset, and the aftermath was catastrophic. Given that a home is almost always a liability, I personally tend to gravitate toward buying assets instead of a home and allowing the assets to pay for my rent or my mortgage on a home purchase. For example, if I know that buying the house I want will cost me $3,000 per month in interest payments or $3,000 per month in rent, I will want to have enough income coming in from rents, dividends, or other Infinity Income to pay this amount.

Roth IRA or Traditional IRA?

Should you invest in a Roth IRA or Traditional IRA? What is the difference, and why are there people converting their Traditional IRAs into Roth IRAs when they subject themselves to big tax hits? The differences are simple: in a Traditional IRA, you are eligible for a tax deduction on monies you contribute to the IRA but are taxed on the withdrawal of contributions and on withdrawals on the gains. In a Roth IRA, you are *not* eligible for a tax deduction on monies you contribute to the IRA but are not taxed on the withdrawal of contributions or on withdrawals on the gains. There are a few rules and conditions on both, but those are the highlights.

- Traditional IRA = Tax deduction now but pay taxes later
- Roth IRA = No tax deduction now but pay no taxes later

That is why some investors get excited by Roth IRAs, because they could contribute $5,000 now and forgo the tax deduction. In thirty years, if that $5,000 turns into $50,000, they pay no tax. Just remember rule number one, *calculate, calculate, calculate.*

If I am in my prime wage-earning years and am paying in a state and federal combined 30 percent tax bracket, I am essentially receiving $1.30 for every $1.00 I contribute because I am deducting $1.00 multiplied by the 30 percent tax bracket. So I really have $1.00 inside the IRA and saved an additional 30 cents on my taxes. If I contribute $1.00 to my Roth IRA, I will have to pay taxes first ($1.00 times 30 percent = 30 cents), so I would only be able to invest 70 cents into the Roth. In reality, I have $1.00 in the Traditional IRA plus 30 cents in tax savings versus 70 cents in the Roth.

You are actually sixty cents ahead with the Traditional IRA on day one. It takes many years of returns to make up that shortfall, but the Roth growth is tax free, so many people still think of it as the better deal. The experts always say, "But you have to pay taxes on the Traditional IRA withdrawals," which is true but is oftentimes misunderstood.

The problem really comes down to the reality of retirement for the vast majority of Americans. The tax rate drops considerably upon retirement. According to the US Census, the average retiree household and median household (the fiftieth percentile) are both in the second lowest federal bracket, which is currently topped out at 12 percent. Assuming at least a 3 percent state tax, an average household would be, at most, in the 15 percent tax bracket. To illustrate the point, I am going to use this number to extrapolate the numbers as an example even though much of the income would be in the 10 percent bracket.

For this example, you can assume the following:

- Individual, forty years old, federal and state combined 30 percent tax bracket, investing $5,000 each year, making a 7 percent return, for a period of thirty years (retire at age seventy).
- If the individual invested in a Roth IRA, they would have $330,613 for retirement.

If the individual invested in a Traditional IRA, they would have $472,304 for retirement.

Okay. But the Traditional IRA is subject to 15 percent tax, so it is really $401,458 with the tax hit. So reality is far different than what the experts tell you. That is why God invented the calculator—it is like your own handy-dandy lie detector.

That same calculator will tell you that Roth IRAs are awesome for young people who are already in the lowest tax brackets as we know their tax brackets will only go up. We also know that a contribution to a Roth IRA can be removed at any time without penalty, so they are excellent savings plans. What almost never makes sense is when someone who is in a higher bracket now than they will likely be in retirement forgoes the tax benefits of a Traditional IRA and puts money in a Roth IRA. There is also something called a conversion where someone takes a Traditional IRA and converts it to a Roth IRA and pays the taxes on the monies converted. This rarely makes sense, in my opinion, yet I see it being done all the time and actively encouraged by many advisors.

Zero-Percent Credit Card

That 0-percent-interest credit card, is that a good deal? It depends on what you're buying. If you're buying an asset, it's a fantastic deal, *as long as you pay it off*. The 0 percent is for a limited amount of time, and then the interest rate soars upward, with the average rate around 18 percent. From my experience almost 80 percent of people who use these cards are carrying a balance at the end of the 0 percent time limit. Then they turn into interest-paying credit cards at the 18 percent interest rate. Not a good deal for you, but a great deal for the credit card company.

They are more than happy to offer it because chances are whatever you're paying with your credit card is a liability. You're either paying for an expense or you're buying a liability. It is not the credit card that is so dangerous, it is what it gets us to buy. The one thing I say over and over in this book is that you should never buy liabilities with a liability.

Stock Selection

You should use the same principle with the stock market. You could put money into a company that's the high-flying stock of the moment, but it's not actually paying you anything. In fact, you're probably paying to have that account open. Or you are losing money because inflation, at about 2 percent per year, is causing the value of your money to go down. So, if you're investing in the stock market, a significant portion of your holdings are not assets. Assets are things that pay you and put money in your account. You should look for stocks like the dividend kings I mentioned in chapter 1. Remember, that is a small group. There are fewer than twenty-five companies that have been paying out dividends for fifty years or longer and have increased the dividend every year for at least fifty years in a row. That growth is something you can actually spend. You can buy groceries with it. That's an asset.

If you bought Amazon when it first came out, you could say, "Hey, it's a high-flying stock. Look, it's gone up so much in value." But it has never paid you a dollar. If you have credit card debt and Amazon stock, you could look at it and say, "Holding that stock costs me eighteen percent." If you paid $10,000 to buy Amazon stock when it was $400, you hit a home run because now that investment is worth $50,000.

You make $40,000 if you sell it. However, there are a few other factors that devalue that return. First, you have to pay taxes. If you held the stock for more than a year, your top rate is 20 percent for federal and whatever your state tax is (we will say 2 percent for ease of use). Now your take is down to $32,000. Then we have to calculate how much interest you paid on the $10,000. Let's assume we held the investment for five years while you had credit card debt or other loans. Average US credit card rates are 19.02 percent in the United States according to WalletHub's Credit Card Landscape Report.[9] If you made no payment and paid the loan back when you sold the stock, you would pay $23,883.60 (the $10,000 plus interest for five years). Of that amount, $13,883.60 is interest, so you would have to subtract that from what you made, bringing your return to $18,116.40 for one of the best stocks in the history of the market. While it is a great return, it is certainly not what you would expect from one of the greatest success stories in the history of the stock market. For every Amazon, there are thousands of failures that take not only your investment but also the cost for interest.

You do not buy speculation with debt. You do not buy liabilities with debt. You do not buy liabilities with liabilities.

It should be noted that these same rules apply to rental properties and rental real estate. Is the investment providing a positive cash flow to you, or is it taking money out of your pocket each month? Is the cash flow paying for any debt that's on it, including interest? Because if you have an asset and it pays for the liability, that makes sense. If it is not paying for the debt on it, then you are paying for it. You are back to carrying buckets. As long as you're not carrying water buckets to the village cistern to pay it, then it's not a liability.

INFINITY NET WORTH

If your bucket-carrying has to pay for something, then it is a liability. I'm not talking about the acquisition; I'm talking about the continuing ownership of it. Is it bleeding you every month? In order to figure that out, you calculate. I'm not someone who is going to tell you not to buy a nice car or a nice house. I'm going to say that if you're going to do that, you have to have an Infinity Income that will pay for it. If your want is to live in a nice house, then you better have assets to pay for it. What are those assets? What do they produce? They produce your Infinity Income, and I'll show you how to calculate that. Infinity Income is income that comes in regardless of whether you are on vacation or working, sleeping or awake, or in the United States or traveling. What we have to do is determine the types of assets that generate Infinity Income.

For example, if you are renting out property that you own, you have to pay attention to your net—what you actually make. Remember that I told you the rule of thumb on a rental property is that about 50 percent should go to your bottom line. If you're renting out a property for $1,000 per month, your expectation is that you are going to bring in about $500 per month after paying for costs like insurance, taxes, repairs, and management. Your monthly net rents would be $500. This is an asset.

You also might have royalties. Maybe you wrote a book, developed some software, or created a video game. Those are also assets. You would calculate any positive cash flow from those as well.

What about dividends? Let's say you own some Coca-Cola stock, and they pay you regular dividends. You own some AT&T, and it pays you dividends too. So does Exxon, Verizon, any of the dividend kings. Now you have dividends coming in and you break it down to a monthly basis. Dividends are generally paid out quarterly, so you have to divide it by three. Or just look at the annual amount and divide it by twelve to come up with a monthly amount. For this example, let's say you earn $150 per month on dividends. These are also assets, and you would calculate the cash flow from them.

What if you have loaned out money to other people? You are also going to include the monthly interest that you are earning. You loaned money to Uncle Ned, and he's paying you one hundred dollars in interest every month. Loans to others are an asset, and any interest you receive should be added to your cash flow.

There are actually three different ways to make money on a stock. Most people only know one—waiting for the stock to go up in price. In order to understand and utilize the other two, you have to understand two simple concepts. First, whenever you own an asset that people want, there is likely an option market for it. An option is a fancy way to say an agreement to either buy or sell it. For example, if you own real estate, someone may want to buy it from you and offer you money for the right to buy it at a certain price for a certain period of time. Maybe you would sell your house for $200,000 and someone says that they would like the right to buy your house at $200,000 at any time over the next thirty days. They say they will pay you $1,000 for the option to buy your house. The longer the period of time, the more they will pay. Second, if there is a market to buy an asset, there is likely a market to sell that asset. If you know you want to buy a particular house for $200,000, you might be able to sell that person an option that obligates you to buy the house for $200,000 for a period of time. For example, you might say to the property owner, if you pay me $1,000, I will agree to buy your house for $200,000, no matter what happens in the market, during a specific six-month period. If the market drops and the house is only worth $190,000, they can make you pay $200,000 for the house. If the market stays the same, you get to keep the $1,000. If the market goes up, you get to keep the $1,000. But if the market goes down, you are obligated to pay the amount you originally agreed to.

In the stock market, the option to buy a stock is exactly like the option to buy a house at a set price. This is called a *call option*, and there are markets for these. We will go over this in detail in later chapters when we discuss renting your stock. The option for someone to force you to buy at a certain price is called a *put option*, and it is exactly like the example above in which you sold the homeowner the right to obligate you to buy the house for $200,000. When you sell these types of options, they are treated as short-term capital gains. This gain is also added as monthly cash flow, and you would need to calculate it in your gains.

The money you have coming in from selling options will typically be a little bit more than the dividends you earn from a stock. If you earn $150 in dividends, let's estimate that you have $200 coming in from short-term capital gains (also known as *option income*). You just add all these up. You have $10 in royalties from the book you wrote a long time ago. You have $500 in net rental income. You have monthly interest from Uncle Ned of $100, and you have monthly short-term capital gains. You add all those up, and it amounts to $960 per month. Great, that's all you do. You're just calculating how much monthly Infinity Income you have coming in.

TABLE 1: INFINITY INCOME EXAMPLE	
Monthly Net Rents:	$500
Monthly Royalties:	$10
Monthly Dividends:	$150
Monthly Interest:	$100
Monthly S.T. Capital Gains:	$200
Total Monthly Infinity Income:	**$960**

CALCULATE YOUR DAILY INFINITY INCOME

Now I'm going to show you how to use this information. You're going to take your monthly Infinity Income and turn it into annual income by multiplying it by twelve months. This number is your annual Infinity Income. However, we want a daily figure for Infinity Income, so you divide the annual amount by 365 (days in the year), and that's going to tell you how much, per day, you earn in Infinity Income.

In the example above, that figure is $31.56 (see calculation below). It is important to calculate your per day amount because if you realize that you're spending $300 or $400 per day and only bringing in $30, that is a real eye-opener for people. It might make someone realize, "All right, maybe I don't need to have six lattes. I can start cutting back."

If I'm spending $400 per day, the monthly income coming in from my Infinity Income sources needs to be $12,167 per month or $146,000 per year ($400 per day times 365).

TABLE 2: DAILY INFINITY INCOME	
Total Monthly Infinity Income:	$960
Multiply by 12 (months):	$11,520
Divide by 365 (days):	$31.56
Daily Infinity Income:	**$31.56**

Our spread is the difference between what I spend on a monthly basis and what I make in Infinity Income. Trust me, this is about as real as it gets.

KEEPING UP WITH THE JONESES

Let's look at the Jones family as an example of how to use this concept. Here are some facts about the Jones family.

They make a total of $7,500 per month from all sources of income. They spend $6,500 per month. Within their monthly income, they have two rental properties that gross $1,500 per month with a net of $750 per month. They don't have any royalties. They do have a nice stock portfolio and have dividend income of $250 per month.

They have $100,000 in a brokerage account and earn zero in interest because they do not loan money to anyone. They used their brokerage account to become a stock market landlord, so they're generating about $400 per month extra for doing nothing other than knowing what to do as a stock market landlord. In other words, they are generating about $1,400 per month in Infinity Income (see calculations below). To arrive at the daily Infinity Income number, we just multiply that $1,400 by twelve months, divide it by 365 days, and end up with $46 per day. That's how much money they have coming in on a daily basis in Infinity Income. So, if they could live on $46 per day, they'd never have to work again because they have enough passive income to cover their needs.

TABLE 3: JONES FAMILY	
Monthly Net Rents:	$750
Monthly Royalties:	$0
Monthly Dividends:	$250
Monthly Interest:	$0
Monthly S.T. Capital Gains:	$400
Total Monthly Infinity Income:	$1,400
Total Monthly Other Income:	$6,100
Total Monthly Income:	**$7,500**

Now we have to determine their spread by calculating how much they spend. They are making $7,500 per month in income from their job salaries. They have expenses of $6,500, so they have $1,000 left over after expenses.

This is called *net income* by most banks.

If they just keep doing what they're doing, they will have an extra $1,000 at the end of the month. The Joneses talked and decided that they could cut their spending an additional $900 by eliminating some of their wants. That $900 is what I often refer to as *fat*. If they took the $6,500 and subtracted the $900, their needs would drop to $5,600. That's what they *need*. Their monthly spread is $1,000 for wants and $1,900 for needs.

Why is that important? Because it informs some critical decisions for the Joneses. We know that they will spend either $6,500 or $5,600. We're going to multiply each by twelve months and divide by 365 days. That's going to tell them how much they need—and we're going to do this both for wants and needs. First, we're going to look at their daily wants. Then we're going to see if there are places where they could trim the fat to calculate their actual daily needs. If they were in a pinch and they had to cut back to survive, they can see that number.

The Jones family has a monthly income of $7,500 and current monthly expenses of $6,500 based on wants. And remember, they decided they could trim $900 of fat from their expenses if they had to. That makes their monthly net income $1,000 based on wants and $1,900 based on needs. So we multiply $6,500 by 12 months—$78,000. Divide that by 365 days, resulting in $213.70. That is what they are spending per day for their *wants*. This is the number most people prefer to use for living the way they want to live versus scaling back.

What if the Joneses did cut back? Right now they're spending $78,000 on an annual basis, or $213.70 per day, for their wants. What is their shortfall? They have Infinity Income of $46.03 per day, so their shortfall is the difference between those two amounts, or $167.67. This is the Infinity Income they would need in order to quit working if they did not want to cut back, and now they have a target for wants. But knowing that they could scale back is helpful, as it lessens the gap quite a bit. Their *needs* amount is $5,600 per month or $67,200 per year. The Joneses thus *need* to spend $184.11 per day. The difference between what they *need* to spend and how much Infinity Income they already have coming in is $138.07.

It is only logical then that the fastest path to reaching Infinity is to do two things: lower the amount of money you spend on a daily basis and increase the amount of Infinity Income coming in.

TABLE 4: JONES FAMILY WANTS VERSUS NEEDS

	WANTS	NEEDS
Monthly salary income	$7,500	$7,500
Monthly expenses	$6,500	$5,600
Monthly net income	$1,000	$1,900
Annual expenses	$78,000	$67,200
Daily expenses	$213.70	$184.11
Infinity daily income	$46.03	$46.03
Shortfall	**−$167.67**	**−$138.07**

If the Joneses were unable to work, their daily burn would be the shortfall amount of $167.67, based on the way they are living right now. This shortfall number allows them to calculate a total number of days that they could survive without working.

Assume they have total assets of $500,000 and total liabilities of $250,000. Their net worth then is $250,000 (assets minus liabilities equals net worth).

They would take $250,000 (their net worth) and divide that by their shortfall amount of $167.67. The result tells them that if they used up their entire net worth by spending every penny of it, it would last 1,491 days without them working.

Let's use a different example. Let's say you're a millionaire with exactly $1 million in assets. Congratulations! According to the world, you are rich. But are you?

Unfortunately, you have no Infinity Income and you have daily expenses of $400. You can reverse engineer this one pretty quickly. You multiply $400 per day times 365 days and end up with $146,000 per year. Divide that by twelve months to calculate monthly expenses of $12,000. Monthly expenses with zero Infinity Income equals a shortfall of $400 per day. How many days could you survive, Mr. or Ms. Millionaire? Divide your million by the shortfall amount of $400. You could last 2,500 days, or 6.8 years. After that you are flat busted. You have had to sell everything you owned, and you haven't a penny to your name. But wait, you thought you were rich! This happens repeatedly for people in retirement; only it isn't so clean.

The problem with selling off assets is that it's never that easy. There are market fluctuations, broker fees, Realtor fees, taxes, and other expenses that can substantially reduce the amount you receive. If you haven't worked for years and your money is gone, you would have to sell everything in a fire sale just to eat. And if that's real estate or a house full of furniture, you're going to have to settle for fire sale prices—usually just pennies on the dollar.

TABLE 5: HOW LONG YOUR ASSETS WILL LAST	
Assets: $1,000,000	$750
Infinity Income: $0	$0
Daily expenses: $400 (times 365 days)	$250
Annual expenses: $146,000	$0
Daily Shortfall Amount: $400	$400
Number of days assets will last: 2,500 (6.8 years)	**$7,500**

What's your Infinity Net Worth? You can go to InfinityInvestingWorkshop.com and use our free calculator to determine your number. You can also use the above process by using your own numbers to determine the number of days you could go without working. It might be depressing to you right now, but if you follow your Infinity Plan, you will eventually hit Infinity. You may start off slow, but you can get there. It's just math. The whole idea is over time we want to get to the point where we never have to sell anything to survive and your Infinity Income just goes on forever.

If you look around, you can see public examples of Infinity Income making huge impact. I work in Las Vegas in a building named for Howard Hughes. He started a foundation that is one of the largest on the planet, worth over $20 billion. Last year they donated over $500 million to medical research. Hughes started his foundation by making a large contribution that grew and compounded because the principal was protected. I call people like these *stewards*, and you will learn more about that in chapter 8.

You can do this with your family as well. If you have Infinity Income being created and you keep building it, and then your heirs don't cash it in when you pass away, it's perpetual. It won't be reduced, and it will continue to grow over time. Statistically speaking, that will turn from $1 million to $10 million, to $20 million, to hundreds of millions. Think extreme. If you go forward three hundred years from now, which might sound crazy, your efforts now have the potential to sustain generations to come.

Chapter 7
Three Losing Bets That Keep You in Financial Prison

John and Sally did everything they were supposed to do. They both had good jobs, they had a nice family, and by all outside appearances were extremely successful. They decided to buy a house, so they met with their Realtor. The Realtor took them straight to the mortgage broker to determine exactly how much house they could afford. Shortly thereafter they bought a beautiful house in one of the best neighborhoods in town.

They immediately began paying off this house and had paid off roughly half of it when the recession hit. Sally lost her job, but John did not. And to be honest, Sally really didn't mind losing her job. She wanted to spend more time with their kids, and she felt like they were in a pretty secure position. As the foreclosures started to happen around them, they didn't pay too much attention because, after all, John and Sally had a ton of equity in their property.

When their neighbor across the street put up the For Sale sign, John and Sally walked across and asked him why. The neighbor explained that they simply could not afford the payments and it did not make sense to keep making payments on a mortgage that was more than the value of the house. So John and Sally asked the obvious question: "What have you set as an asking price?" His answer shocked them. It was substantially less than what John and Sally believed the houses were being sold for in their neighborhood and was about half of the mortgage amount that still existed on John and

Sally's own home.

John and Sally started getting anxious and thought it might be wise to see if they could get back some of the money they had paid off on the house. They contacted their mortgage broker and asked him if it was possible to refinance their home. After all, the rates had gone down since the recession hit. Their broker told them it would not be possible because they no longer had equity in their home. You see, equity is based on that value of the home minus any debt. So even though John and Sally had paid off half of the original debt on their home, they actually had no equity because the value of the home had dropped.

He had more bad news. The interest rate on their mortgage was being adjusted, and their payment was actually going to go up. The massive disconnect for John and Sally was that they had always assumed that the equity in their home was what they would leverage to send their kids to college and use when it was time to retire. So, rather than putting the money into savings, they had been paying down the mortgage of their home, and now that money was gone. John looked at Sally and breathed a sigh of relief knowing that at least he still had his job, and if the mortgage went up, Sally could always work to make sure that they could continue to be current on their debt.

Six months later the increased payments had finally taken their toll. Sally realized that despite all of her experience and her best efforts, there were no jobs in their area that would pay her what she was used to making. John and Sally realized that they'd have no choice but to sell their home and get out from underneath the hefty mortgage. So they did something called a *short sale* and were able to walk away from their home without owing any money to the bank. They lost all of the money they had put into the house—all of the extra payments, everything. And again, they realized that as lousy as it felt to lose their house, they were lucky to get out.

THE THREE BIG INFINITY NOS

In the previous chapter, you learned how to use the Infinity Calculator to convert your old-style financial information into new Infinity numbers. Now we're going to focus in on some aspects of personal finance that have caused many people a lot of pain in this country. There are three losing bets that are guaranteed to keep you in financial prison. In this chapter we will review these losing bets, and I'll show you how to avoid them.

We are going to build off of the lessons you leaned in chapter 5 about calculating your income, expenses, assets, and liabilities. Let's examine how these things interact and learn what the biggest mistakes are that people commonly make when they misunderstand how these categories function together.

There are three major financial mistakes that people commonly make. I call these the three Big Infinity Nos. We will review them and examine how your income statement and balance sheet interact, and it's all about the flow of the money. For example, if you are simply working and paying your expenses and don't have any extra money to go into assets, this is what the flow would look like.

INCOME/EXPENSE STATEMENT	BALANCE SHEET
INCOME	ASSETS
EXPENSE	LIABILITIES

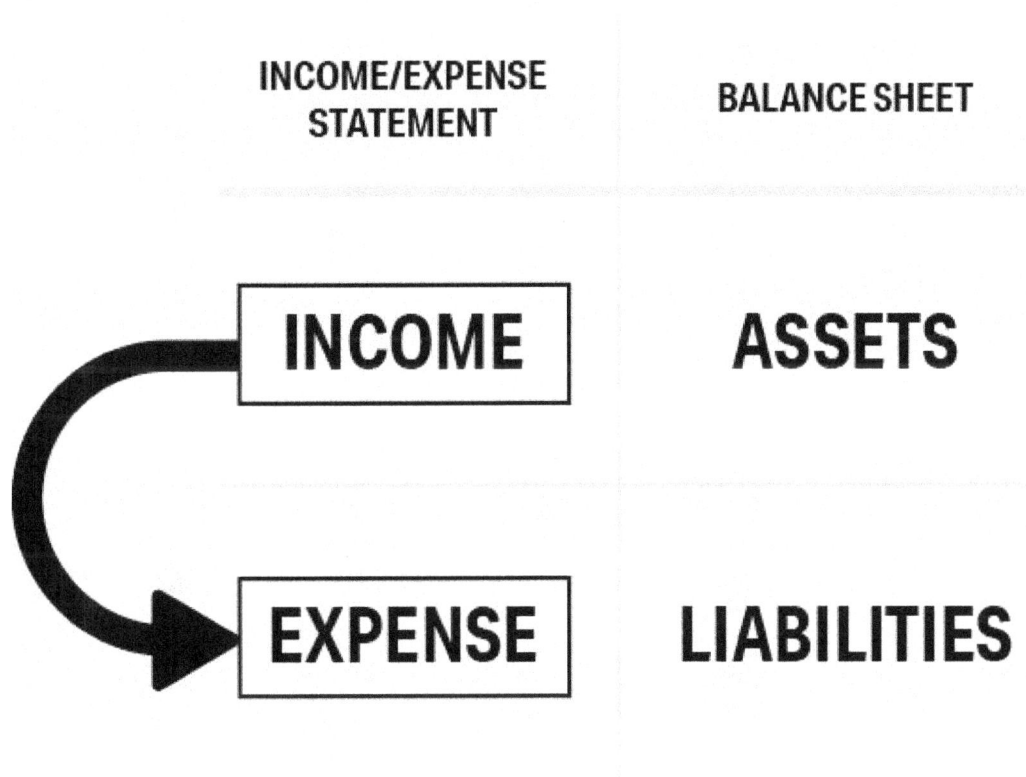

That's pretty simple, but our financial lives aren't that simple. There are some traps that are easy to fall into. The first Big No is *do not pay expenses with liabilities*. An easy example to understand is don't use credit cards to pay your rent. You would incur a liability to pay an expense, and if you do this, it's absolutely going to be a problem.

Big Infinity No Number One: Never Pay an Expense with a Liability!

INCOME/EXPENSE STATEMENT	BALANCE SHEET
INCOME	**ASSETS**
EXPENSE (RENT)	**LIABILITIES** (CREDIT CARD)

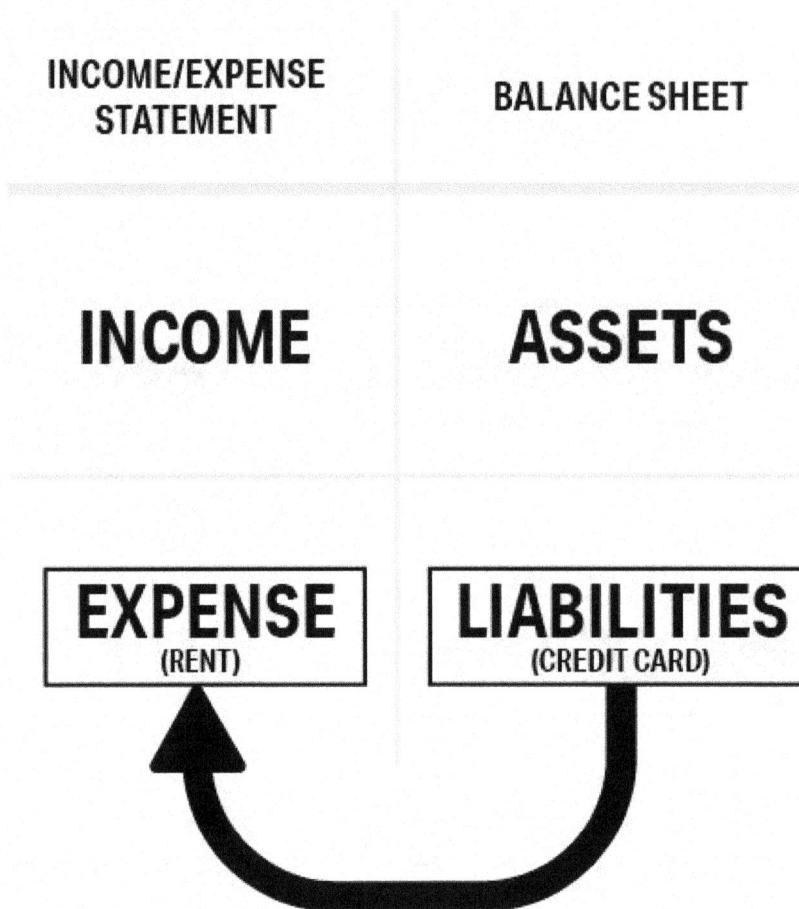

I understand that some of you might say, "I have no choice." You always have a choice. Cut the expenses; get that number down. Work your tail off to not incur liabilities to pay for your expenses. Just say no. The only exception to this one is if you're a college student and you're going after an engineering, professional, or other degree that has a high market value that you can verify. You can see the starting and average salaries of dentists, for example, and use those data to make reasonable calculations. History, philosophy, English, or similar degrees are hard to track and have low average salary values. In general the starting wage for an English major is going to be somewhere between fifteen dollars and nineteen dollars per hour. It makes no sense to incur substantial debt for this type of degree. If you're incurring a small amount of debt, I get it. But if you are a working-age adult and you're working full-time, absolutely, positively, 100 percent do not pay an expense with a liability.

Big Infinity No Number Two: Do Not Buy Liabilities with Your Income!

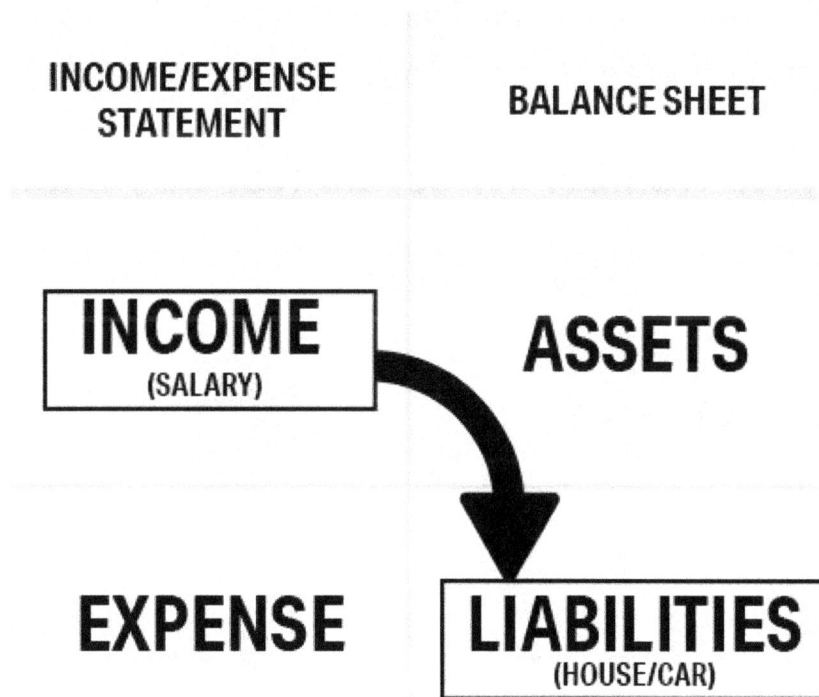

INCOME/EXPENSE
STATEMENT

BALANCE SHEET

INCOME
(SALARY)

ASSETS

EXPENSE

LIABILITIES
(HOUSE/CAR)

Resist the temptation to buy something just because you financially qualify. First-time home buyers are often surprised that they qualify to buy a big house. That doesn't mean they can afford it. This is often the start down the road to pain. Your real estate agent would love to sell you a more expensive home because they make more on the commission. Lenders would love to max you out to make money off of you on the loan. Credit card companies love it when you buy things on your card and carry a large balance. The furniture store salesman would love to sell you new furniture for each room of your house and will likely have in-house credit to offer as well. As a result of these scenarios, you end up in financial imprisonment. It is as if the lenders are all thinking, "Let's see if we can't put you into servitude so that we can make some money off you."

Do not buy liabilities with your income. Buy assets with your income. When you have enough assets, you can start in with larger purchases, but not before. This is a game of Monopoly. Your first several times around the board, you buy assets that will produce income later. This is not the time to spend lavishly just because you want stuff.

Big Infinity No Number Three: Do Not Buy Liabilities with a Liability!

INCOME/EXPENSE STATEMENT	BALANCE SHEET
INCOME	ASSETS
EXPENSE	LIABILITIES (HOUSE/CAR) (CREDIT CARD)

You might think a car loan is pretty safe, but Big Infinity No number three is do not buy liabilities with a liability. So, as an example, let's look at something many people do—buying a car with credit. Don't do it. You need to have an asset that is paying for that car. Let's say I have a rental house that's generating five hundred dollars a month positive cash flow, and I get a car loan that is five hundred dollars a month. Okay, that's fine. I am not incurring extra expense. I'm paying for it with earnings from an asset.

The same is true of boats, RVs, or anything else that is a want and not a need. This is even true for your home. To add clarity, there is a base reasonable expense for just about any need. For example, I need transportation, probably a car, but I do not need a Bentley. My base transportation will be a certain dollar amount for a basic car. Everything else is a want. Whatever you do, do not buy the want on credit. Do not buy a want by taking out a loan.

Let's make this real. If you know you can rent a reasonable home in a reasonable neighborhood for $1,500 per month, then that should also serve as your budget for buying a home. This is not just the mortgage payment, but insurance, interest, maintenance, and all the other added expenses of a home. Everything is a want, and you should avoid using a loan or credit to pay for that want. What you should do is rent the reasonable home in the reasonable neighborhood and build up assets with any extra money you can save. As those assets increase, your ability to buy liabilities with the cash flow from those assets increases. At that point you might be buying a liability, but you are no longer the one paying for it. The asset is paying for it.

THE LOSING LOOP: RIGHT THIS WAY TO PAIN AND SUFFERING!

I have been talking about the Losing Loop for years and used to just teach it as a recommendation. But things have progressed to make this something akin to a national crisis. The rich are getting richer, and what's left of the middle class is being pushed down. This is how they are doing it to the rest of us, and it can only be defeated with honest assessment and deliberate avoidance. This is the rat race, the hamster wheel, or the golden cage. Whatever you call it, this is how so many people find themselves in the abyss of financial prison, yet it is easy to avoid.

If you violate the Big Infinity Nos, you will find yourself in the Losing Loop. Here is a simple explanation. The Losing Loop is when you are working to pay off liabilities but you are not earning enough to pay your expenses and pay off your liabilities.

As a result, you have to incur more liabilities to pay for your expenses. Your liabilities grow, you have no assets, and you end up with an increasingly negative net worth. Eventually, no one will give you more credit and you will find yourself either in bankruptcy or on the street. And yes, it can happen to anyone.

If you do go out and buy a car with a loan, a home with a mortgage, a degree with student loans, or a bunch of great furniture on your credit card, you end up in the Losing Loop. The Losing Loop is the direct path to massive pain and suffering. The Losing Loop costs people their health, their marriages, and sometimes their lives. Don't believe me? In America, the average wealthy person lives twelve years longer than their poor counterpart.[10]

The problem this loop creates is that you're working your butt off just so you can have more liabilities. You're carrying buckets, paying your credit card bills, mortgage, student loans, real estate taxes, and car loan. You keep buying and paying your credit card minimum, and you have nothing left over. And because you have nothing left over, now you have to put some of your expenses on your credit card, and your balance is going up every month.

```
        INCOME/EXPENSE
           STATEMENT            BALANCE SHEET


    ┌──────────────┐
    │    INCOME    │─────┐        ASSETS
    └──────────────┘     │
                         ▼
    ┌──────────────┐   ┌──────────────────┐
    │   EXPENSE    │   │   LIABILITIES    │
    └──────────────┘   └──────────────────┘
            ▲                   │
            └───────────────────┘
```

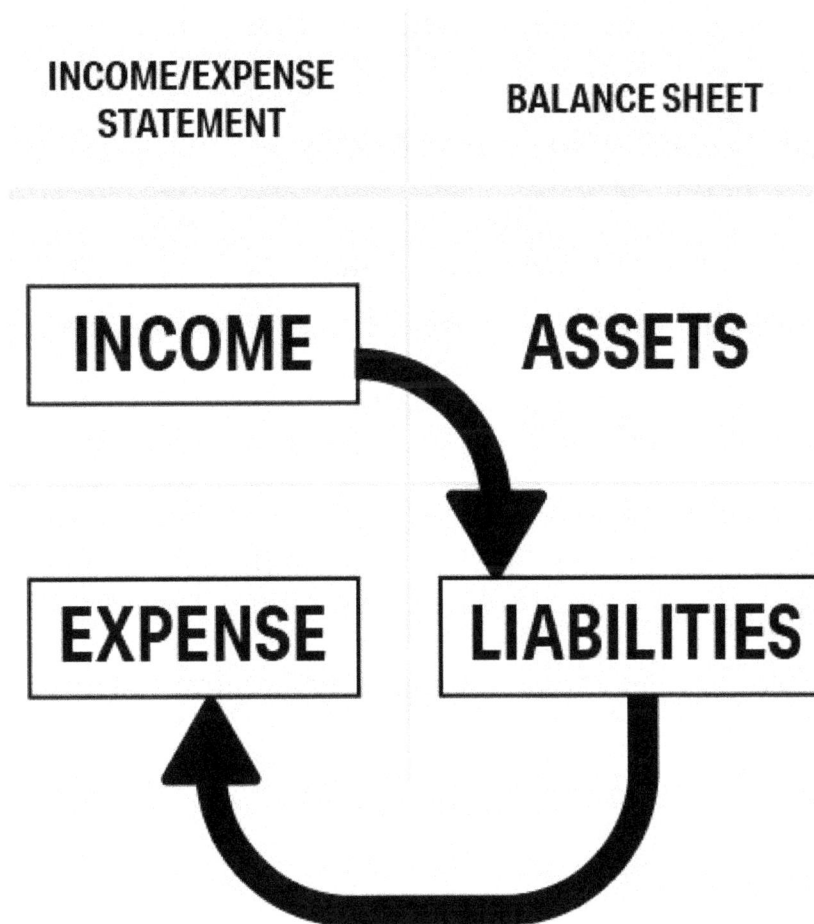

You might say, "Oh, I don't do that." Well, I see it all the time. The vast majority of Americans are experiencing some sort of financial turmoil, and this is often the scenario they're in. And they've convinced themselves that they don't have these liabilities—that these are assets that they're buying— yet they're losing their shirts. When I see their bank statements, it's obvious. And quite often, they'll actually have temporary amnesia and forget that they have liabilities. "Oh, I forgot about my student loan. I forgot to consider that I have a car payment. It is so small. I didn't even think about that credit card. It has a really small balance." That's a bunch of crap. You have to be brutally honest with yourself and count everything. Not doing so is what causes the pain and suffering. This is what causes divorce. This is what causes health problems. This is what causes people to lose hope. This is what causes so many problems with abuse of alcohol and drugs, suicide, you name it. It comes from this lack of hope caused by the vicious cycle of the Losing Loop. And if you find yourself in this trap where you cannot pay your expenses, you're incurring liabilities to pay your expenses. You feel like you are working for someone else's wealth and that you are in financial prison. I want you to avoid this like the plague. The way you do that is to avoid the three Big Infinity Nos.

Big Infinity No number one—do not pay expenses with liabilities. Just say no.

Big Infinity No number two—do not buy liabilities with your income. Just say no. Buy liabilities with assets instead.

Big Infinity No number three—do not buy liabilities with a liability. Just say no.

Do this and you avoid the Losing Loop. The Losing Loop is nothing but pain and suffering. And if that sounds preachy, so be it.

Chapter 8
Three Keys to Breaking Free

Charlie was driving home from work one day and listening to the radio. A financial expert on the radio was telling people not to buy nice cars, to live in really small homes, and to save everything they could for their retirement. People would call in, and they would get berated for wanting nice things, as according to the host they didn't need them. Charlie was thinking to himself, "I kind of like nice things—am I a bad person?" He thought, "There are certainly excesses in this world, but I don't think that having a nice car is one of them if you can afford it." He turned off the radio for the rest of the ride home.

The following weekend Charlie and his wife were invited to a party with a bunch of their friends. When they arrived, Charlie saw one of his very successful friends who drove nice cars and always seemed genuinely happy. Charlie explained what he had heard on the radio, and the friend commented, "The radio host probably perceived nice cars as being expensive and a waste of money, so they thought that nobody should have nice cars. If he thought big houses were excessive, then nobody should have a big house, and if having nice things was, in his opinion, excessive, then nobody should have nice things." The friend added, "What a horrible world we would be living in if that were the case." Charlie asked the friend what he thought the radio host's real point was. The friend said that we all suffer from the habit of putting our pocketbook into the pockets of others. In other words, "Because they couldn't afford these things, they believed they were excesses."

Charlie thought a lot about what his friend had to say. There are people who will never understand how somebody might want to buy a Ferrari because they assume that it is too expensive for that individual. In the radio host's mind, they would have to work so hard to pay for that Ferrari that it would never be worth it, so no one should buy a Ferrari. Charlie kept thinking over the following week and realized the same could be true for cell phone, shoes, clothing, and just about anything else that would be considered a discretionary purchase. How about food? Should you ever go to a nice restaurant ever again?

Shortly thereafter Charlie found himself driving and listening to the radio host again. The host was telling someone they should eat macaroni and cheese for dinner every day to save money. It was at that time that Charlie vowed to never listen to the radio host again.

AVOID THE CRABS

Charlie's story plays out on a daily basis in the United States. Many adults are unhappy and express their unhappiness by complaining about a system they believe is rigged or unfair by telling anyone who will listen about their plight. I call these people "crabs" because of their instinct to pull other people down with them. If you have ever been crabbing, you will notice that crabs refuse to work together to escape a bucket. In fact, they do the opposite— they pull each other back in when one crab is about to escape. When a person is a crab, they tend to tell you all of the things you cannot do and why you will fail. They get an almost perverse sort of pleasure at stopping others from following their dreams.

Interested in investing in the stock market? The crab will tell you that you will lose all of your money and it is nothing more than a racket. Interested in opening a business? The crab will tell you 90 percent fail in the first year. Interested in investing in real estate? The crab will tell you that everyone lost their shirts in the great recession because of real estate.

You get the picture. Crabs are quick to discourage others, and their facts are almost always 100 percent wrong. These are the same people who will tell you only greedy people drive nice cars. That only selfish people own nice homes. They will impose their views on you and assert their experience as being divine wisdom with which they are only trying to help you. What they are really doing is sharing their misery because misery loves company. If they can keep you in the bucket, then they will not feel so bad being in the bucket themselves.

The truth is that escaping the bucket is easy, especially if you have help. If you were a crab and stuck in a bucket, whom would you ask how to escape the bucket? The crab who is also stuck in the bucket, or a crab who has escaped the bucket? Of course you would ask the crab who has escaped. Unfortunately, most people these days live in the bucket and cannot stand it when people escape. Believe me, if you want to escape the bucket, do not listen to the advice of those stuck around you—listen to the advice of those who escaped and help other people escape every day.

As someone who has escaped the bucket, I would advise you to think about nice things this way. It is okay to enjoy nice things, but you do not want to have to work needlessly hard for those things. Instead, you want to buy assets that will generate enough money to pay for the nice things. Quit thinking of a Ferrari as something that you have to work for to buy. What you have to work for is the asset that will then generate enough income to pay for the Ferrari. Let the asset buy the Ferrari, and you can have as many Ferraris as you want. You're not actually buying a Ferrari anymore; you're buying an asset that pays for the Ferrari.

This is no different than CEOs having a nice office, a nice company vehicle, or access to the company jet. If there's a profit motive behind it, it's deemed okay in corporate America. By comparison, having something nice in the personal realm is often judged a sin. I'm not trying to judge your use of your assets. My only point is that you shouldn't be using your labor to pay for a nice car. You shouldn't be using your labor to pay a mortgage. You should buy assets that pay for those things, and then the amount of that mortgage or the amount of that car payment becomes immaterial because you are not working for it. Your assets are.

If somebody walked up to you and said, "Hey, I'd like to provide this nice Mercedes for you, and I'll pay all the bills and everything. Heck, I'll even pay the taxes that you would owe on it." Would you tell them no, or would you simply tell them thank you? What if you work for a nonprofit and someone there said, "Hey, we have company cars, and they just happen to be really nice cars because we get a really good deal at the dealership and they practically give them to us." Would you refuse to drive it? In other words, is it the car you're objecting to or the price of the vehicle that you're objecting to? Because if you're not objecting to the vehicle, by all means, drive it; the price is immaterial if you are not paying for it. If your assets (like your rental properties, for example) are paying for the lease or the car payment, go ahead. Or, if you saved up the income from those assets and you're using that pile of cash to pay for it, then it isn't your labor paying for it. That becomes a much more palatable situation.

Now, some of you would never want a Ferrari, and to those of you I'd say, "Cool, I don't want one either. I'm much more comfortable in a truck." But I would no more tell every one of my clients that they have to buy a pickup truck then I would tell them that they shouldn't buy a Ferrari. I just say, "If that's something you want, make sure that you have assets that are paying for it." I would no more tell them that they have to live in a home that's fifteen hundred square feet versus telling them that they should not live in a house that's ten thousand square feet. I would say, "If that's what you are doing, make sure you have assets to pay for it." It's a different way of thinking, but it makes all the difference. Besides, when you can afford things, they often become less and less desirable.

If you follow the rules set out in Infinity Investing, you will not have to worry about working to buy nice things ever again. That is because your purchases will happen in the right order. It is no different from getting dressed in the morning. If you have a habit of taking a shower, drying off, and then getting dressed, it seems very simple. However, if you reversed the order and got dressed, dried off, and then took a shower, you would be all wet. The order in which you do things is vital.

This is exactly how it works in finance and is especially true for Infinity Investors. Wise people buy an asset, allow it to pay expenses, then allow it to pay liabilities. It is simple and seems easy to people who follow the correct order. If you reverse the order and buy a liability, use your income to pay expenses, and then try to buy assets afterward, you will find that you have nothing left over with which to buy assets. You are all wet. Understanding the correct order and following the rules—which we will be covering next—is not only important but also easy. As easy as getting dressed in the morning.

RULE NUMBER ONE: USE INCOME TO BUY ASSETS

INCOME/EXPENSE STATEMENT	BALANCE SHEET
INCOME ➡	**ASSETS**
EXPENSES	**LIABILITIES**

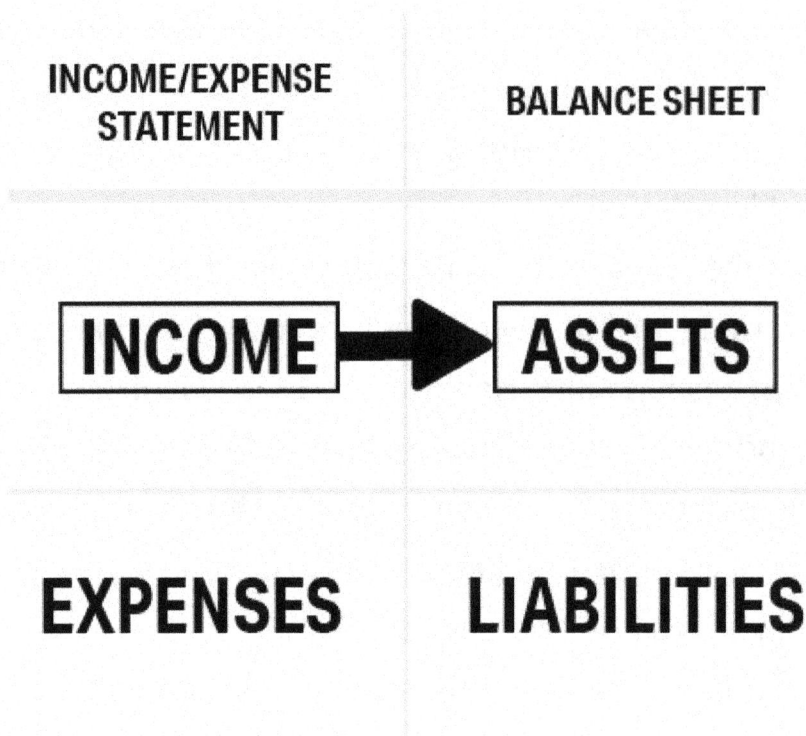

First, we're going to follow rule number one, and it is a simple rule: use income to buy assets. The idea is to use your income to buy things that are going to feed you. Before you say, "Hey, I can't afford some kind of expensive asset"—you're assuming that I think you should go out and buy a bunch of rental properties—or "Well, I am barely meeting my expenses. I can't loan money to anybody," if that is you, start small. You could just buy a few shares of stock to get yourself started. You can open a commission-free account on Robinhood, for example. It will take you all of about fifteen minutes to fill in the information. It takes a couple of days for them to approve the account, and you could then buy a dividend-producing stock right away. When you buy something that pays out a dividend, you now have an asset. Now you are following rule number one. You are using your income to buy assets.

You still might be saying, "Well, hold on for a second. I have all these expenses." Okay, not a problem. In that case, you can tap into your spread. Take the portion of your money that you're not spending and put it toward an asset that will kick off some income to you. So again, you could start building an income-producing portfolio of assets that are going to be the things that eventually pay for your expenses. At first you will be in the accumulation phase. You will be putting your money toward buying these assets. It's also possible that you will choose to take the money that the assets make and continue to buy assets with it. You are just going to keep snowballing until you have a base of assets, but the first step is to commit to using your income to buy assets, not liabilities, first.

RULE NUMBER TWO: USE ASSETS TO PAY EXPENSES

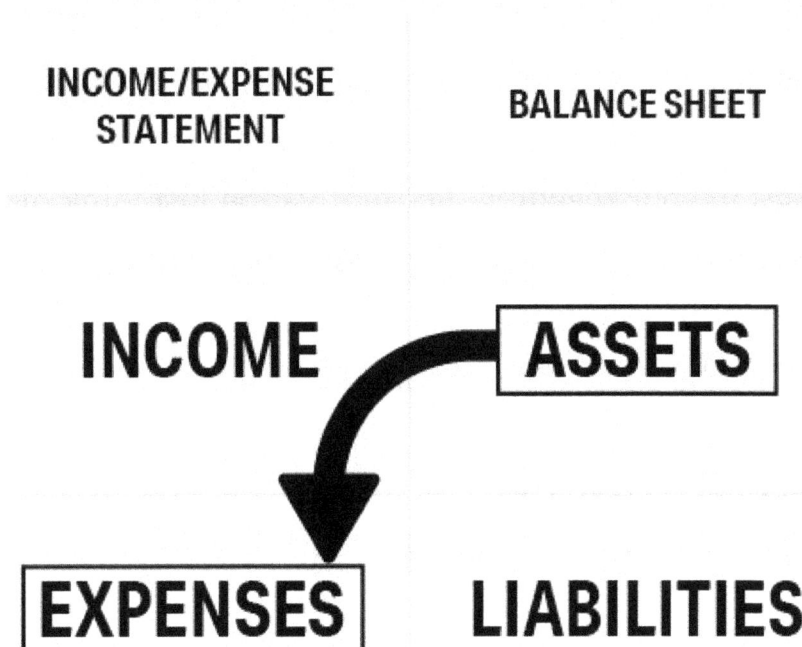

INCOME/EXPENSE
STATEMENT   BALANCE SHEET

INCOME → ASSETS

EXPENSES   LIABILITIES

The second rule is to use your assets to pay your expenses. Remember, these assets include things like rents, royalties, interest, dividends, and short-term capital gains. You use your assets to cover your needs and your wants. This is the point where you will take a hard look at your wants. I'm not going to tell you to reduce your lifestyle, with one exception. If you are already in the Losing Loop, you will have to change your lifestyle in order to make

Infinity work for you.

But if you're not in the Losing Loop, you have a bit more latitude. I'm not going to tell you that you shouldn't go to Starbucks. I'm going to strongly urge you to be very smart about it and make it a priority to build up your asset base. If, instead, you spend on an expensive want (probably a liability), you will likely regret it and think in hindsight, "That was a waste of my money. I should have redirected that money into an asset." This is particularly true the closer you get to building up enough assets to cover your expenses.

It is this step that might take the longest for people, as your wants and needs tend to grow over time, especially if you have a family. However, if you remain committed to rule number one and continue to invest in assets, those assets will also continue to grow as well, and often at a pace that exceeds increases in your spending. For motivation just think of the day when work becomes voluntary. The day when you have enough income coming in from your portfolio of stocks and real estate that you can cover all of your needs. That will be the point when working is your choice.

RULE NUMBER THREE:
USE ASSETS TO PAY FOR LIABILITIES

INCOME/EXPENSE STATEMENT	BALANCE SHEET
INCOME	**ASSETS**
EXPENSES	**LIABILITIES**

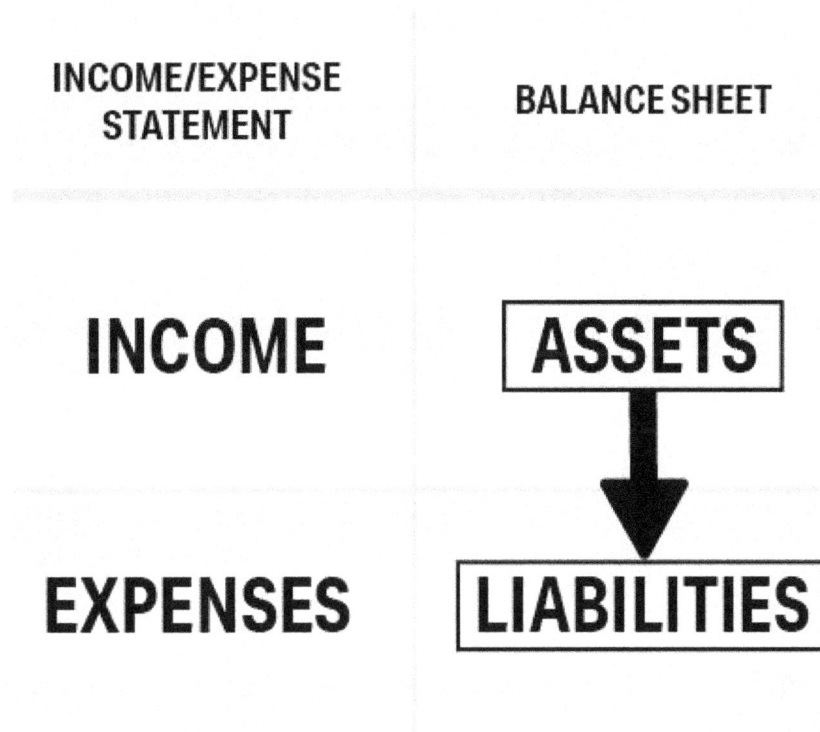

Rule number three is use assets to pay for your liabilities. If you want to drive a Maserati, I'm not going to tell you not to buy it. The Infinity rules say that you need to have some income-producing assets to pay for it. If you want to have that super house, let your assets pay the mortgage. Let your assets pay for any loans or for your lease payment.

I'm not trying to keep you from having things you want, as long as you don't have to work all day carrying water buckets to the village cistern to have them. Build your pipeline to pay for them. That way you have the water flowing in by itself. Following this rule will create a flow of money coming in on a monthly, quarterly, or annual basis. Use that to buy a big house. Go for it. You want to use that to buy a big car? Go for it. Make sure there's enough water coming through that pipeline to cover the expenses associated with those things so that you don't have to pay for it out of your income. Your assets will pay for it.

If you're not there yet, just continue to accumulate assets until the assets can provide enough money to cover it. If you look at how the top 2 percent use their money (and remember, you're getting whacked by taxes when you earn that money), they're earning the money and immediately putting it into assets that produce Infinity income. In a rental property, for example, they know that they may not have to pay tax on the money that they make because of this thing called depreciation. They're writing off the purchase of the rental property against the income, so they may not have to pay taxes on it. The way to think of this is as follows:

If I earn one dollar carrying buckets, I will get to keep seventy cents for every dollar I make because I have to pay, on average, thirty cents in tax. That is because employees *earn* money, then *pay tax* and *spend* leftovers.

If I earn one dollar from the pipeline, I get to keep that dollar. This is because businesses and investments *earn* money, *spend* the money, and *pay tax* on the leftovers. In many cases the tax paid by the investment is a fraction of the tax you pay on money earned working. For example, if I earn $40,000 in one year, my federal tax rate would be as high as 12 percent. Make the same $40,000 as dividends and you pay 0 percent. You will almost always have more buying power when you have investments versus making money working.

If you follow the path of building assets, all of a sudden you have a lot more money because it's not being taxed as high as your salary or wages. You use those assets to pay for your expenses. And while it's paying for any of the liabilities that you have, you can do something called leveraging the asset. That's where you start putting a liability against the asset (for example, a line of credit or loan) and use the money to buy more assets that compound and continue to grow and grow and grow. The important thing here is to always calculate your return and make sure it is positive if you use leverage. It is a very effective tool, but it can hurt you if you are paying more for the leverage than it is generating. So always calculate, but do not lose sight of the power of leverage when buying cash-flow assets.

THE IMPACT OF HOLDING ASSETS

When compounding causes assets to grow, it starts off slowly, then gains momentum, and then grows very steeply. This is called exponential growth, and it always occurs with compounding asset growth (see illustration).

Notice the difference that just 10 years can make on on a $1,000 investment

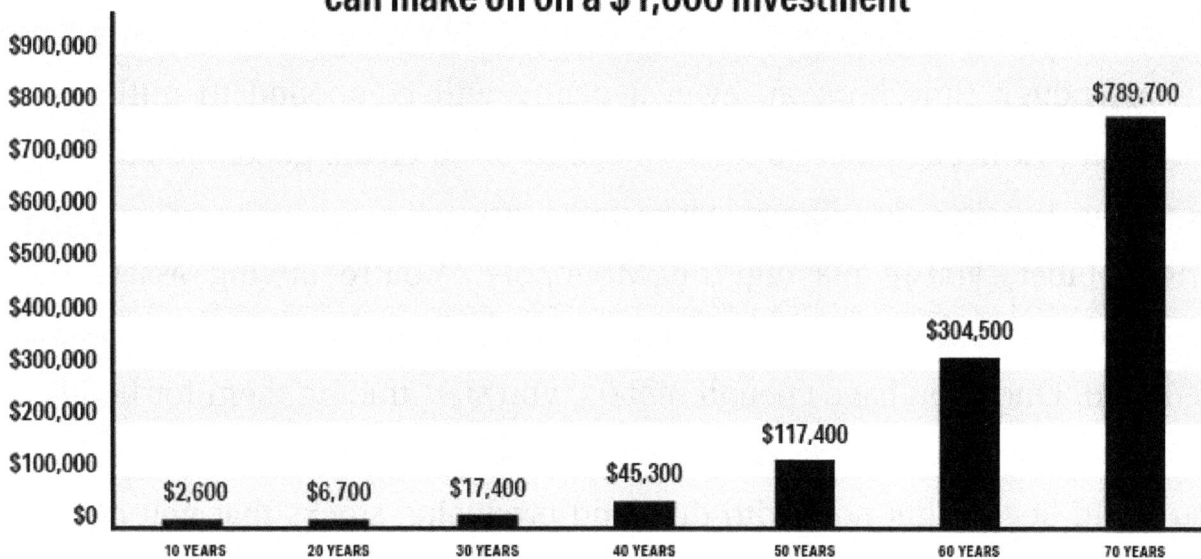

10 YEARS	20 YEARS	30 YEARS	40 YEARS	50 YEARS	60 YEARS	70 YEARS
$2,600	$6,700	$17,400	$45,300	$117,400	$304,500	$789,700

$1,000 compounding at 10%

The longer you hold, the greater the compounding. It only makes sense to hold onto your assets for as long as possible. The problem that many families have is with the intergenerational transfer of that compounding asset. For example, Mom and Dad are saving, saving, saving, and they're building toward the path where steep compounding builds the asset. The value is going up, the parents hold onto the asset and, at some point, inevitably pass away. We generally have about thirty years between generations. And what will typically happen is then the heirs have a sell-off, and—*boom*—the exponential growth is not only stopped, but usually sidetracked into spending. The sell-off of Mom and Dad's assets causes their value to be depleted, and the proceeds are often spent frivolously. The assets usually never make it to the point of the extreme growth phase.

If Mom and Dad started early enough or they do not allow their heirs to sell off the assets, they could get there, and that's part of good estate planning. There is a responsible way to grow wealth to so that it doesn't get depleted, grows steeply, and provides revenue as an asset. I call this the 200 Year Plan; it centers on the idea that compounding will necessarily create exponential growth if given enough time no matter what you start with. Over a long enough time horizon, even a penny will compound to millions of dollars; it just needs time. So all we need to do to create generational wealth is an asset and time, just like an acorn and a tree.

Remember, you're playing life Monopoly. You're buying assets first. You're using your money to buy rentals during your first few times around the board. Once you have enough rentals, you start trading them for hotels or whatever other assets Monopoly makes available to players. In the real world, you could begin right now with dividend-producing stocks that you can buy for less than a hundred bucks to get started. If you wanted to buy one share tomorrow, you could do it for zero transaction cost with Robinhood. You could start doing these things immediately to produce income and apply that money toward your expenses.

Instead of working your tail off to pay for your mortgage, car, student loan payments, or high-interest credit cards, you have assets that generate enough income to make any payments. You use your assets to buy the liabilities and then you work hard to buy more assets. This is what wealthy people do. The two-percenters, they're taking their income and buying assets. Then they use those assets to pay for their expenses and pay for their liabilities.

Just think about the previous paragraph and the sentence that included "working your tail off to pay for your mortgage, car and student loan payments." Change it to "working your tail off to buy an apartment building." Do you see a difference in those two statements? In one case, you are working to pay someone else. In the other, you are working for your own benefit.

Here is another way to express it: "Jordan worked double shifts for a year to earn enough money to make the payments on his loans." How does it make you feel about Jordan?

Now consider this: "Jordan worked double shifts for a year to earn enough money to hit one million dollars in his brokerage account, and that kicked off enough dividends that Jordan never has to work again."

Does it feel different? Jordan is working his tail off in both sentences, but in the second sentence, you go from feeling bad for Jordan to feeling perhaps a bit envious. In the first sentence, we see that he is in servitude, compared to the second sentence where we see Jordan is achieving a freedom. As human beings we all strive to be free and instinctually know the difference between servitude and freedom. All we are doing in Infinity Investing is giving you the keys to the cell.

THE BEST TIME TO START IS RIGHT NOW

I cannot drill this in hard enough. If you have to go back and read this twenty times until you grasp it, make sure you are getting this. You're taking your money, and you're immediately investing in something that's producing what you need to pay for your expenses. If you don't have enough money, then I'm going to show you step-by-step how to get there.

In a conversation I had with our CEO at Anderson Business Advisors, David Gass, we discussed a financial planner that we both knew. A married couple in their early forties came into his office. They were earning about

$40,000 per year, and they wanted to retire. The financial planner said, "There's no way," but then he looked at their numbers. They owned rental properties that were more than paying for their expenses, and they lived pretty frugally. They didn't have any debt. They owned their house outright. They owned their cars outright. They did not have children, so they didn't have those related expenses. They had enough assets and did not need to work. The planner was kind of shocked and asked them how they had done it. They said that they just always put 20 percent of their money aside into an investment account, and when it got big enough, they would buy another rental property.

That is the secret. Remember what you just read about a penny turning into a million dollars over a long enough time horizon? Well, this is exactly what they did. They consistently put money into assets and allowed the investments to compound. They did not increase their spending as they generated wealth. They made sure that they increased their investing and purchased more assets until they had enough money coming in that they did not have to work unless they wanted to.

I'm not necessarily telling you to just go buy rental properties; I'm just saying that's what they did as part of their plan. They were not earning huge salaries, but one thing they did brilliantly was to not worsen their position. An excellent speaker I know and respect asks her clients to think about what position they were in when they were eighteen. She asks them if they had debt at that point in their lives. When you were eighteen, I'm guessing you probably didn't have any debt. Were you in a better financial position then than you are now? In other words, what's your net worth at that point? You might say zero because you didn't have any assets and you didn't have any liabilities. Fantastic. Where are you at now? Are you negative or positive? Have you done better since you were eighteen, and how much growth do you have? If you have positive net worth, how much per year have you accumulated? You can figure this out by dividing your net worth by your age minus eighteen. For example, if you are sixty and you have a net worth of $500,000, you have managed to accumulate $11,905 per year since you were eighteen. How does that relate to what you have earned per year?

Unfortunately, many adults are underwater. They lie to themselves about what an asset is, and they overvalue the property they have. They think, "Well, I can always sell my car for twenty thousand dollars." No, they sell it at a fire sale, and they maybe get $7,000. They have to sell their house but have never taken a hard look at the comps to have a realistic sense of the actual value on the market, not to mention taxes and transactional costs. You should take a critical look at everything to see whether or not you actually have positive net worth.

Some of us walk around thinking we have a high net worth just because we have accumulated a lot of stuff. Yet if we actually make the effort to calculate, we see that mathematically we were better off when we were eighteen. The whole idea is not to go backward. From this point forward, you will be able to do an accurate Infinity assessment. If you start doing this today and really work this program, one year from now you'll be able to see how much extra Infinity Income you have. You will be able to see that you have reduced your expenses because you start to pay attention to them. You will have paid attention to your spread and your shortfall, and you will be able to see if that's getting bigger or smaller. What is most interesting is that your net worth becomes less and less relevant, and what becomes ultimately important is how much Infinity Income you are generating and how much you need to spend.

When you start cutting into the shortfall, then it's just a matter of time before you reach Infinity. It will happen because it is a mathematical process if you follow this direction. It is just like climbing a mountain. As long as you are going up, eventually you will reach the peak. As long as you're reducing that shortfall and you're increasing your assets, you are going to hit Infinity.

Chapter 9
Serfs, Apprentices, Knights, and Stewards

There once was a young boy who lived in a foreign land with his mom, dad, and older brother. Together, they moved to the United States to seek out better opportunities. While he had only managed to complete a few years of schooling, he got a job in the United States at a cotton factory. He made $1.20 per week at the cotton factory. He was only thirteen. He never went back to school.

Over the years the boy worked very hard and held several different jobs, eventually getting a job as a telegraph messenger. The boy would watch and learn how the telegraph operators worked the telegraph and worked his way up to becoming a telegraph operator himself. He was transferred to a railroad company and repeated the process of learning and doing hard work with similar results. He was just eighteen when the company promoted him to a management position.

The boy watched the successful people around him and did what they did —he invested in various businesses. He understood that there were lessons to be learned from the successful people around him and that they were willing to help. Over the years the investments grew and more opportunities surfaced. He was becoming wealthy.

The boy, who was now a man, noticed that there were opportunities in the burgeoning expansion of railroads. He began investing in projects benefiting from the railroad expansion, including everything from bridges to steel.

Eventually, he founded a steel company that grew enormously. He sold it for hundreds of millions of dollars and dedicated the rest of his life to helping others achieve success.

The boy was Andrew Carnegie.

FOLLOWING THE PATH

Up to this point, you have learned everything you need to know about how to do the calculations for your Infinity Plan. Now we're going to take a look at the behind-the-scenes class system involved in personal economics. If I told you there are four classes that we can divide people into—serfs, apprentices, knights, and stewards—where do you think you would fall?

In this short but critical chapter, you will learn the difference between the classes, how to define them, and then how to determine which class you belong to. I will talk about moving from one class to another later, but first let's determine where you are.

SERFS

In medieval times, a *serf* was someone bound to the land in service of another. It was a form of indentured servitude where the serf and the land were generally bonded. The owner of the land was the lord, and the serf worked the land in exchange for a home and some money. The income from the serfs was used to pay knights and cover the other expenses of the lord.

For our purposes, serfs are those people who don't have enough passive income or Infinity Income sources to cover their needs. For these folks the loss of a job can be devastating. So can an illness or any other surprise expense that throws them into flux, like quarantines and shutdowns. These folks have been sold a bill of goods. They are often the ones who bought a big car with big monthly payments or a big house with a big mortgage, and now they feel like they're on a hamster wheel. We call people in this category serfs because they are earning money that serves someone else. If you remember how net worth is calculated (assets minus liabilities), you probably now realize that a liability you are holding may be an asset to someone else. The assets are held by the banks, credit card companies, car loan agencies, or mortgage institutions. The liability is held by you, and it is often a struggle to keep up. We're going to figure out whether that's you or not.

Just like the serfs of medieval times, serfs today tend to be at the mercy of others. Their jobs are at the pleasure of another, their homes are owned by others, their independence is dependent on someone else. In an instant life can change and turn the world upside down for the unprepared serf.

APPRENTICES

The medieval *apprentice* was someone committed to learning a trade and going through the stages of becoming a master. In short, they were on the path of being excellent at a given trade. They were generally supported by another person but were granted support with the understanding that they were on a path to becoming a master. They almost always had the favor of a knight and were expected to become one themselves over time.

In the Infinity system, the apprentices are folks who, if hit with an unexpected expense, can survive. They are in a situation where their basic needs can be covered, no matter what, by a certain amount of passive income. If they have to, they could cut back some on their wants and still live in a reasonable fashion. They have enough of an income coming in to cover all of their needs; they would just need to dial back on their wants to make it through.

KNIGHTS

Going back to medieval times, *knights* were highly sought after because of their skill and code of conduct. For their service, they were given land and sums of money because they understood and excelled at the craft of battle.

Let's set aside the medieval context for the moment and look at these roles in terms of Infinity Investing. Knights have learned how Infinity assets work and no longer need to work for themselves. Knights have managed to cover both their needs and their wants. They have reached Infinity on the Infinity calculation of net worth, and they can do what they want to do. They can basically live off of their Infinity Income indefinitely.

Knights often will have several apprentices because knights love to share the joys of knighthood. Knights are the ones you often see campaigning for the apprentices and serfs while trying to lead them to freedom. Because they do not have to work but know how to, they really enjoy challenges and making a difference. You will also find knights working tirelessly on matters they believe are very important. You will notice that knights become focused more and more on their legacy and on helping others throughout their lives.

That is not to say there are no bad knights who do destructive things out there. But the bad ones tend to be the exception to the rule. The bad knights usually have no stewards (we'll learn about these in a moment) and are nomads, drifting with no real purpose or values. In medieval times these were the mercenaries or hired swords who had no purpose other than to fight. There is still hope for them, of course, if they determine what is important to them and strive to become stewards. Almost all knights have the ability to transition to stewardship if given enough time and a strong desire. In fact, it is not uncommon for knights to have children who also join the knighthood with the plan to become stewards.

STEWARDS

Finally, *stewards* are those who have enough to cover all of their needs, wants, and wishes. Stewards often become the philanthropists who spend most of their time helping others because it is rewarding for them to do so and because they have the means to do it. People like Andrew Carnegie and Bill Gates have been a couple of the most visible, but there are millions of people who, after obtaining Infinity with enough excess wealth to buy pretty much anything their hearts desired, turned to helping others as a way to gain fulfillment. These people have stacks of money but spend stacks to help others. Look what Bill and Melinda Gates have done with their foundation. Warren Buffett, the Oracle of Omaha, has an estimated net worth of $72 billion. He has pledged to give 99 percent of it away. These are true stewards.

You might say, "But wait, everybody makes a contribution to society in some way." But it is the stewards who are the people that make the huge differences with wealth. Consider Andrew Carnegie. He was the wealthiest man on the planet in the early 1900s. He wrote an article in 1899 called "The Gospel of Wealth." It was published in *The North American Review* and stated his opinion that millionaires are trustees of the poor. He said that the self-made wealthy had a responsibility to not squander their money on extravagance and to not even necessarily pass it all to their heirs. Rather, they should use it to help society be stronger. Late in his life, Carnegie's net worth was estimated to be $470 million (probably $14 billion by today's value). When he died in 1919, he had given away most of this fortune to charities. He believed that if you were good at making money, you owed it to society to make as much of it as humanly possible, then use it to help others. It was an argument that capitalism was inherently better than other systems because it created an incentive for people who were the best at something to continue to excel at it.

Put another way, with the proper incentives in place and societal pressure to use money to benefit society, everyone in a capitalist society is better off, no matter how much money they make. No matter how you look at society, the person who is worse off in society today is almost always far better off than their counterpart was a hundred years ago. Innovation allows us to not look at capitalism as a bad thing. If you're good at making money, you should do it, but you should make sure that you're giving back to society. The problem is that oftentimes there are insufficient incentives in place to promote giving back. Bill Gates and his Giving Pledge initiative is an excellent example of how someone with wealth and an incentive to help society can actually put pressure on wealthy counterparts to dedicate giving most of their wealth back to society.

I call that a steward, somebody who's contributing back to society in a very different way. Carnegie built libraries, which he described as a ladder to accomplish something you may have thought was out of your reach. If you wanted to reach up and grab it, you could pull yourself out of your current situation. It was a place dedicated to making information available to anyone with the motivation to change their station in life, which is exactly what we're doing with Infinity Investing.

Milton S. Hershey is another example of a steward, and I often use him as an example in estate planning. He did not have children of his own, but in 1910 he created The Milton Hershey School to provide cost-free education to orphan children. To this day the school maintains a K–12 enrollment of two thousand students. The Hershey Trust, which owns the school, is worth over $13 billion because it continues to compound. The school is just one of a number of local and national charities funded by the foundation for the benefit of society—all created by a man who wanted to help others. That is what I call a steward.

One more steward example is Howard Hughes. In 1953 he founded the

Howard Hughes Medical Institute from the profits from the Hughes Aircraft Company. It's the fourth largest charitable foundation on the planet and is the single biggest steward for biomedical research. Hughes was an unusual and secretive individual. It was after he was passed that his legacy grew and the fortune compounded to become what it is today.

So that's a steward—someone whose needs, wants, and wishes are met so that they can contribute back to society in some meaningful way. Some choose not to, but in my opinion that is a missed opportunity and is unfortunate. If you have ever met someone who was truly wealthy and still angry and unhappy, there is often a link to the issue of their having missed this opportunity to gain fulfillment. Without proper guidance, wealth can be a curse, so it is extremely important to identify why wealth is important to you.

WHERE ARE YOU?

Let's review these one more time so that you can better understand where you might fit as of right now. The easiest way to understand it is that a serf is somebody whose Infinity Income is less than their needs. If you're at zero, you're a serf. You don't have Infinity Income, and your starting point is to begin to build it up. If you have enough Infinity Income to meet your needs, but less than enough for your wants, then you're an apprentice. You're getting there.

Once you have enough to meet your needs and your wants, and you have enough to cover your lifestyle as it is right now, you are a knight and you are just focusing on making sure that you can meet your wishes. You have enough passive income from the Infinity Income sources like rents, royalties, dividends, and short-term capital gains. You can do what you want to do. At this point you might say, "What do I wish I'd be able to do? I'd like to be able to travel the world. I'd like to be able to do some other things."

Fantastic. Your wishes are met. Now you're giving back to society. You owe it to society. Become a steward with your wealth and success.

In the next chapter you will learn the specific actions to put into place so that you can change your station. I will focus in particular on helping those of you who are serfs or apprentices to become something we call a *stock market landlord.* If you are a steward or a knight, you're ahead of the game and have figured out how Infinity Investing works. Your challenge going forward will be to help others, so for you we are going to be focusing on how to help those who are serfs and apprentices. Then I will present a ninety-day plan with concrete action steps to follow.

Chapter 10
Where the Wealthy Invest

There's an inmate in San Quentin Prison named Curtis Carroll who teaches stock trading and is known as the "Oracle of San Quentin." He has spent most of his life incarcerated and is actually in a stint of doing fifty-four years to life for his part in a botched robbery that ended in murder. So this is not the ordinary person who finds his way to the stock market.

Curtis didn't know how to read when he went to prison, but he taught himself. One day he was reading a newspaper and, believing he had the sports section, was confused by the information listed in front of him. It turned out that he had accidentally opened up the financial section. He asked a fellow inmate what it was, and the inmate's response was "This is where white people keep their money."

The more he studied, the more Curtis realized that the financial markets were available to everyone. In interviews, he talks about reading the *Wall Street Journal*, *USA Today*, *Forbes*, and business magazines and publications all the time and said he couldn't believe that anybody, literally just anybody, could go into the stock market and make money.

He has worked with fellow inmates and some well-known people outside of prison in creating courses to help people understand financial literacy. I think some of his theories deserve mentioning. He says that anybody who's mastered true wealth has mastered four basic steps, which are saving, cost control, borrowing prudently, and diversification.

Curtis was only seventeen when he committed the crime for which he's imprisoned. That in no way forgives the violence or loss of the life of another human being, but he has come to realize that it is the lack of knowledge of finances that leads many into a life of crime, and by helping people learn how to be financially secure, it will help reduce crime. Curtis teaches inmates how the stock market works and, in his own way, creates hope in others.

THE ADVANTAGES OF THE STOCK MARKET

In this chapter I am going to talk about the wealthy, what it is they're really doing with their money and how it is different from traditional investors. We already know they utilize multiple sources of income, as we discussed in previous chapters. Remember that they receive income from things like rents, royalties, interest, dividends, and capital gains. In this chapter we are going to take a much deeper dive into one of my favorite places to make money. It's a place that the wealthy utilize considerably, and it's called the stock market. We're all familiar with the market, but the wealthy use it in a way that most others just aren't quite aware of.

When you look at the numbers, the stock market has outperformed all other asset classes over time. That is really quite remarkable, and there are several substantial advantages to treating the stock market like a business you own.

- First, you don't have to hire employees. This gives you a way to generate income without having to have the cost, regulation, hassle, and responsibilities that can come with managing a staff.

- Second, another unusual advantage that's very specific to the stock market is that you can buy and sell whatever you want. Every stock will always have a buyer and a seller. If you have been previously involved in real estate, for example, this is very different from what you're used to, as there the sale process can be slow and buyers can dry up. That is not the case for major stocks. You can't always dictate the price, but there will always be somebody who is willing to sell stock to you or buy your stock from you. That gives you a lot of unique advantages.

- Third, you can do this anywhere as long as you have an internet connection. You're able to manage your wealth with just a quick online connection and an online broker. No costly offices or the overhead that comes along with having a physical location.

These are just a few of the strong advantages of the stock market, and add to this the fact that it's where we've seen some of the biggest gains overall. Everybody should be utilizing it at some level. What we know with our work with wealthy clients is that they use the stock market a bit differently than the traditional way.

THE TRADITIONAL INVESTOR MINDSET

With traditional investing, what usually happens is that people buy stocks that they like and that they know, and then they hold on to them. Nothing wrong with that thinking because for the most part it does work—as long as you have money to invest and a long window of time. And this is where traditional investors can get into trouble because it takes time and the markets must be going up to make this work. Let me give you an example using the S&P 500, which measures five hundred of the largest companies listed on exchanges in the United States. The S&P 500 is a big overall exchange that gives us an idea of what the markets are doing. It is a very commonly used benchmark, and it fluctuates greatly with the economic conditions of the time.

A lot of mutual fund managers and hedge fund managers set as their goal to beat the S&P 500. If you looked at a graph of performance over time, there would be a number of peaks and valleys. You would see that the S&P 500 was up during the tech bubble heading into 2000. Then we went in to the 2000 crash when the markets tanked and tech stocks really dropped. Then we rallied into a real estate bubble in 2007. After that we saw the 2008 real estate crises and subsequent big market crash. Then the chart climbs back up as a result of what is often referred to as the Fed bubble. There was a lot of quantitative easing (printing money), and a lot of what was happening was inflating the markets—some would argue artificially. Nevertheless, things were moving back up.

Then after the latest presidential election, there was another really big surge in the markets. Then came the COVID-19 crisis and its aftermath, and an enormous crash. Then a recovery where almost all of the gains came from six of the five hundred companies. That shows you the up and down nature of the stock market. Again, traditional investing really is a sound strategy if you buy and hold and have time. The problem was if you were someone who invested in stocks and had planned to retire in 2000 and wanted to pull that money out and pay for your living expenses for the rest of your life, you were in a world of hurt. Why? Because we saw a substantial drop in the market, and stocks that you had planned to cash were worth so much less than they had been a mere six months earlier. After that crash the markets rallied again into the real estate bubble. On that next rally, it was fine because the markets came back. So, for the long term, as long as you didn't sell your stocks, you were okay. But then the market crashed again, and we went through another cycle.

I want to be very clear on this point so there is no confusion. The problem with buying and holding for the long haul only is that when the stock is sold to help pay for retirement, medical expenses, or any other purpose, the market could be at a low. You cannot go to the electric company and say, "Hey, my stock just dropped twenty percent; can I pay my bill when the market comes back up?" No, you have to pay the bill now, when the market is crashing, and it can cost you dearly.

It is the nature of the stock market to have rallies and crashes and rallies and crashes. It's just the way stocks move. They fluctuate over time. Knowing this, and if you're the traditional investor counting on pulling cash from the market in one of these years that happens to be an off stock market year, you could end up really being in trouble as a result of your traditional strategy. If you research the crash of 2000, you see it took a full thirteen years before the markets came back to the level that they were at in 2000. And that's where the traditional investor and even traders get in trouble because they're trying to time the markets. Don't get me wrong. To some extent timing can be useful in the markets, but it proves counterproductive over and over again. Consider the fact that according to S&P Dow Jones Indices, after fifteen years only 92 percent of funds actually beat the S&P. In 2019 only 29 percent of fund managers beat the S&P. These are "experts" at timing the market, yet they fail more often then they succeed. It makes no sense to pay someone who will more likely than not lose you money compared to the S&P.

Let's think about those thirteen years during market recovery. That's a pretty long period of time, though I may think, "Well, for me as an adult, over the entire span of my life, thirteen years isn't that long." But look at your children and think about how different their lives are going to be in thirteen years. They may have graduated from college, found a job, and be well on their way. Think about what they have the potential to accomplish in thirteen years. Think about you and your money, and what you want to accomplish. When you think of a traditional investor that had to sit and wait for more than thirteen years before their money came back and surpassed where it was in the year 2000, it's a pretty depressing thought, isn't it?

I can promise you that there were some people who were making money in those thirteen years. Sure, some investors just held on and waited. There were also people who sold at the bottom of those crashes, and it was disastrous. But there were others who really knew how to handle the markets and knew the opportunities that are there every day, and they used them to generate cash throughout those thirteen years. What is it that they were doing, and what do they know that you don't?

HOW THE WEALTHY USE THE STOCK MARKET

What the wealthy don't do is sit around and wait. They utilize dividends and stock rentals to increase their wealth. They buy stocks at a discount, earn dividends, leverage those dividends, and also receive rent checks on their stocks. These four things are very important in the stock market and can open opportunities for you. What this boils down to is that the wealthy, instead of trying to just make money on an upswing in a stock like a traditional investor does, focus on doing things to lower their risk. They want to eliminate the chances of losing a bunch of money in the market.

How they do that is by using the stock market as a cash-flow vehicle. This is a critical fundamental of how the wealthy invest. They are not just trying to make money on the big upswings in the market. They have an approach for generating cash using the stock market as the vehicle. What this could do for you is allow you to step off of the roller coaster of those markets. As I mentioned earlier, the stock market is going to go up and go down over time. The S&P 500 will rally, then sell off and then it will rally again and sell off and then rally and just keep going. Overall, the S&P 500, as with all of the major US indexes, has continued to grow over time, but not without ups and downs. It is with all these ups and downs that traditional investors can get hurt if they don't know how to handle them. By trading and investing like the wealthy do, you're going to be able to avoid getting hurt by those swings and generate consistent cash flow. And then your stocks just become a vehicle for growth. What's great about it is that your stocks will bring in quarterly, monthly, sometimes even weekly cash flow right there for you.

The secret is that they never have to sell stocks to pay for things they need. They are never forced to sell a stock when the market is crashing. They have taken the time to understand that certain stocks are assets that create cash flow, and they understand how to use that cash flow to compound their growth. In short, they look at the market differently than most of the so-called experts and turn it into a cash-flow machine.

FOCUS ON DIVIDENDS

What you need to do right off the bat is start looking at purchasing stocks that pay dividends. A dividend, as you learned in earlier chapters of this book, refers to a company sharing the wealth. It's a portion of a company's earnings that they pay out to all of their shareholders, and the more established companies are going to be the ones that pay a dividend. So often new companies, like high-profile tech companies, are going through big growth cycles. Instead of paying a dividend, they'll keep the cash and reinvest it to grow the company. They need the cash to acquire other companies or because they are not yet earning a consistent profit. More stable companies that are already established have already gone through a lot of their growth and have consistent profits, so they reward investors by this cash dividend payout and do so consistently.

You may wonder if dividends are for you. Is it even anything worth looking into? As you may already know, cash is not the best place to have your money. Unless it is earning some sort of return, $1.00 at the beginning of the year is worth about $0.98 at the end of the year. This is because of inflation causing things to become more expensive over time. In the United States, average annual inflation is around 2 percent. If you can put your money in something that at least keeps up with the pace of inflation, you're breaking even. By comparison, if you are in cash, you get just behind. Dividends historically are a hedge against inflation. Most companies will end up paying a higher dividend than the rate of inflation, so you're actually getting ahead a little bit on the dividend.

The second thing that I think is even more important and more exciting is that the stocks that pay a dividend typically outperform those that don't. That is because companies that pay consistent dividends over a period of years are operating profitably and can generally afford to continue to pay out the dividend. A consistent dividend over a length of time becomes a really good filter for you. If you know you already have access to a group of companies that tend to perform better than others, why not stick with those to begin with?

REINVEST ON AUTOPILOT

Another thing to keep in mind is that when you have a dividend-paying stock, you have an extra bit of leverage. And if your broker allows, you can take advantage of a dividend reinvestment program (DRIP). A DRIP provides an easy way to automatically reinvest your dividends. How it works is when a dividend is paid out, it goes directly into your brokerage account and is reinvested into shares or partial shares of the stock of the company paying the dividend. As a result, you will continue to grow your stock portfolio. It's great because you don't have to do anything. The dividend reinvestment automatically buys you more of that stock every single quarter. One other option is to do a partial DRIP, in which part of the money is reinvested into stocks and maybe part of the money you keep as cash. Then you can even pull some of that money out as cash on a quarterly basis. But then you've got a vehicle, which is your stock, giving you either more stock or some cash returns. Either way, this is great for an investor. Most brokers do this, but not all, so definitely find a broker that allows DRIP.

Dividends are a compounder of wealth, meaning over time the compounder, along with the original investment, will begin to grow exponentially. For example, in the S&P, since 1929 dividends have accounted for 40 percent of the S&P returns despite averaging between 3 and 5 percent annually. When we look at the dividend numbers, they may look a little bit small, but over time what we get from these dividends can be pretty spectacular.

THE DIVIDEND KINGS

Within the group of companies that pay dividends, there is a very small subset called *dividend kings.* These dividend kings are companies that have been paying out dividends and increasing that dividend every year for fifty years or more. Impressive, right?

Think about it this way. Your Uncle Ned comes up to you and says, "I want you to invest in my company." And you say, "All right, Uncle Ned, I'll give you some money for your company, but I want to receive something in return. Either I'll loan it to you and you pay me interest, or I'll put that money in your company and you pay me a share of the profit. That way I get something back for my investment." That's the old way of investing. You would actually invest money, and you expect to get something back.

Times have changed and investment practices have too—but not necessarily for the better. Consider the group of stocks known as FAANG and made up of Facebook, Apple, Amazon, Netflix and Alphabet's Google. These are some of the most popular and best-performing tech stocks out there. The thing is, these companies don't really pay anything back to the investor. In fact, Amazon lost money for the first nine years before it turned a profit. So you have these companies that just aren't paying out, but people invest in them with the hope that the companies will continue to grow and the stock value will continue to increase. And we've been hoodwinked into believing that it's okay to invest in companies with the idea that they will continue to grow and their value will always continue to go up. Are you willing to take that risk?

Here's a little news flash for you. You can't spend their growth. In order to spend that growth, you have to sell the stock, and if you sell it, you're paying taxes on it. If you're selling it in an IRA or a 401(k), you might think you're not going to pay taxes on it. Well, yes you are, when you take it out. The one exception is if it is in a Roth 401(k) or a Roth IRA. (As an aside, this is what every young person should have. This is a great place to save your money because you'll never pay tax on it, and you can always pull the money out if you need it in an emergency.)

But let's go back to the dividend kings. The reason for putting your money in these companies is because they pay you something for your investment. Consider AT&T. They are currently paying stockholders a dividend of between 5 percent and 6 percent. It's interesting because even as they try to figure out what they are as an organization, they actually pay out a pretty big chunk of money to their shareholders each quarter. You're going to get 5 or 6 percent back just in the dividends that they pay you. This doesn't take into account any growth in value if their stock price increases. They are paying you for using your money, not the other way around. Now who is working for whom?

As I write this, there are only thirty companies that qualify as dividend kings. These are companies like Coca-Cola, Johnson & Johnson, Procter &

Gamble, and Lowe's, to mention a few. What they have in common is that they all pay a dividend and have increased their dividend for at least fifty years. With a little instruction on how to determine appropriate times to acquire a stock, investing in dividend kings can allow you access to a great compounder along with great companies without the risk of chasing the market. All of a sudden, your high-quality investing options are more focused and your investment choices are clearer.

Why would you pay somebody 5 percent or 6 percent to bet your money on stocks when some manager is getting paid every time they buy and sell—what we call churning the account? Why do investors do that? Because they don't know better. What you're going to do is pick companies that are supersafe and have a track record of always paying out. Why would you take a bet on a company that never pays a dividend? You're just giving them a tax-free or an interest-free loan, and you gamble that they will grow while hoping to get your money back in the long run. And if you need your money unexpectedly, you have to sell that company at the going rate and pay taxes on any earnings. Compare this to an investment in a dividend king that is paying you money; you can actually pay bills with the money that it pays you.

If you're not impressed yet, consider this. If you had invested $100,000 at the beginning of 1991 in both the dividend kings list and the S&P 500, the difference would be remarkable. And remember the S&P is the big benchmark that everybody's trying to beat. At the end of that time period, your $100,000 invested in the S&P 500 would be worth $1,370,419. By comparison, the same amount invested in the dividend king list would be worth $3,245,873. Maybe these companies on the dividend kings list don't look really exciting, or maybe you have never even heard of most of them. But are you after exciting, or are you after returns?

THE DIVIDEND ARISTOCRATS

There is another group of stocks to pay attention to as well, and they're called the dividend aristocrats. These companies have been paying and increasing dividends for at least twenty-five years in a row. This list of companies is quite a bit longer. And again, we've got a whole variety of sectors represented: consumer staples, financials, healthcare, material stocks, utilities, information technology, energy stocks, and more. You're probably getting a sense of my enthusiasm for these lists, so you may be thinking, "Okay, I'm ready; I'll jump right in!" But you do want to be a little bit cautious.

Just because the stock is on a dividend king or a dividend aristocrat list does not mean that it pays a particularly high yield (the percentage return based on the stock price). There are quite a few stocks that have a yield of 1.5 percent or less. The lists are a great place to begin, but there are other great companies that have been paying out steady dividends over a shorter period of time that are also excellent. Ten years of increasing dividends with an excellent company may be a great investment, just like fifty years of increasing dividends can be a poor investment if the price is too high. As a result, one of the things you'll use in your decision-making process is how high the yield is. How much cash am I really getting for buying the stock?

That brings us to the critical question. How do you know what a good investment is? How do you know what stocks to buy? It's a little bit of a balancing act. You want some degree of security, meaning you want a safe company that will be around for the long haul. You want to buy this and own it forever. You want to balance it with a good dividend so you get a decent payout and are provided with good leverage. We have a list of seven criteria that we use in our mastermind group to determine if a stock is a good investment and a safe one, and I will go into detail on that in chapter 12. The first step is to learn to read the basic analytics for any stock.

STOCK CHART BASICS

The Coca-Cola Company (KO)

Previous Close	49.83	Market Cap	212.753B
Open	49.80	Beta (5Y Monthly)	0.55
Bid	0.00 x 1100	PE Ratio (TTM)	23.26
Ask	0.00 x 1800	EPS (TTM)	2.12
Day's Range	49.35–50.07	Earnings Date	10/16/2020–10/20/2020
52-Week Range	36.27–60.13	Forward Dividend and Yield	1.64 (3.29%)
Volume	18,445,733	Ex-Dividend Date	9/14/2020
Average Volume	15,659,242	1Y Target Est	53.55

When you're looking at a dividend payout, just know that they're typically paid out quarterly. Let's look at Coca-Cola's chart as an example.[11] You'll notice that there is a whole bunch of information here, including a previous close, the opening price, bid, ask, day's range, volume, market cap, PE ratio, and more. Rather than deal with all of the data, what I want you to look at is the *forward dividend and yield*. That will tell you how much Coca-Cola is paying. What you'll notice is that there are two numbers, $1.64 and 3.29 percent. The first, $1.64, is the dividend, and 3.29 percent is the yield.

Let's talk about the dividend first. By the way, this is an annual dividend, so for every share of Coca-Cola that you own for the year, you will make $1.64. You will be given that check right from the company. Or, better yet, if you use the DRIP program, have that reinvested right back into that stock so that you're just buying more shares. Now, since these are actually paid on a quarterly basis, that means that each quarter you're going to get paid $0.41 for every share you own.

The other piece of information that you see in parentheses is the yield. The yield is a pretty simple calculation. It is just the dividend divided by the current stock price, and you get a percentage. What's more important? Is it the yield or the actual cash that you're getting? It's a little bit of both, because the yield takes into consideration how expensive the stock is. If you have a stock that pays a $0.60 dividend, but it's a $100 stock, your yield is going to be way lower. This gives you an idea of what your return is compared to how much you're actually investing. Most people actually look at the yield over the hard cash that is paid. I like to look at both. I start out with the yield as my filtering factor. It's really nice to get at least a 3 percent yield, but if a company has a really high yield, you may worry if they've been dropping in price and their yield is actually going up. It's something called *high yield danger*.

If we use Ford as an example, and we go back to 2018, Ford was at $18.00. By 2019 they were at $8.00. In 2018 Ford's yield was around 5 percent. As the stock has dropped in price, the percentage yield increased until 2019's 8 percent yield looked spectacular. You could look at that chart and think the high yield looks very appealing, but you worry about the dramatic drop in share value. Instead you opt for a stock that has a lower yield but more stable share price.

While learning about dividends, there are some key terms to know. These are not all on the stock quote but are still important to know. One of them is the *declaration date*. That just tells you the date that the board announces, "Hey, we're going to have a dividend." *Date of record* is the date that the records are reviewed to identify who the shareholders are. The *ex-dividend date,* which is included on the quote, as we will show you in a moment, is the date before which you have to own that stock to receive that dividend, and this is really, really important. If you do not own the stock before this date, you will not receive the dividend. Last is the *payment date,* and that's important because it tells us when we're getting that cash in our account or gaining more shares of that stock by DRIP. But out of all of these dates, the most important is the ex-dividend date. Especially if you don't already own the stock and you're trying to buy the stock to get the dividend, you have to buy it before the ex-dividend date (also referred to as just the X date).

The Coca-Cola Company (KO)

Previous Close	49.83	Market Cap	212.753B
Open	49.80	Beta (5Y Monthly)	0.55
Bid	0.00 x 1100	PE Ratio (TTM)	23.26
Ask	0.00 x 1800	EPS (TTM)	2.12
Day's Range	49.35–50.07	Earnings Date	10/16/2020–10/20/2020
52-Week Range	36.27–60.13	Forward Dividend and Yield	1.64 (3.29%)
Volume	18,445,733	Ex-Dividend Date	9/14/2020
Average Volume	15,659,242	1Y Target Est	53.55

Looking back at the quote for Coca-Cola, let's zero in on the ex-dividend date. If you look at Coca-Cola's ex-dividend date, what you'll notice that it is September 14, 2020. You have to own the stock before September 14 to earn the dividend. Just remember that if you're planning to purchase stock to get a dividend, you have to buy it at least one day before the ex-dividend date (a.k.a. X date). You will receive the dividend on the payment date as published by the company and usually on the company website. Here is Coca-Cola's website posting for its upcoming dividend:

The Coca-Cola Company (KO)

UPCOMING DIVIDENDS					
Ex-Div Date	Amount	Frequency	Payment	Record	Announced
9/14/2020	$0.41	Quarterly	10/1/2020	9/15/2020	7/16/2020

So now you are clear on what a dividend is. You know how the yield is calculated and you know what it tells you. You're going to use these as your criteria to filter stocks. You know what date you need to have ownership of the stock in order to collect that dividend. At this point all of that might not sound very exciting to you.

A $1.64 dividend for owning a share of Coca-Cola stock for an entire year? If you own a hundred shares of Coca-Cola stock, you make a whopping $164. Okay, by itself, it doesn't sound that exciting. But I guarantee you, over time, the extra $164 per year keeps compounding. Coca-Cola has raised its dividend fifty-seven years in a row, meaning Coca-Cola has increased its dividend payout for fifty-seven straight years, not to mention the increase in its stock price.

THE POWER OF DIVIDENDS

Coca-Cola has been paying dividends since the early twentieth century and has increased its dividend payout over 2,300 percent since 1988, as well as continuously increasing its dividend for more than fifty-seven years. Right now Coca-Cola pays out more than $1.60 per year per share, but if we go back and see just how much of an impact the compounding of dividends has on returns, we might consider that in 1988 they paid 7.5 cents per share.

This does not seem a very big amount, and yet a bunch of really smart financial people, including Warren Buffet, invested. By 2020, here we are at $1.64 a share. That is what you get with this compounding growth of the dividend and the automatic reinvestment through DRIP. The power of compounding given a long period of time gives you extraordinary results, and this is what wealthy people use to grow their portfolio and grow their wealth.

Compare that strategy to traditional investors who buy good stocks and hold them but have no compounder. They hope that their stocks increase in price so that someday they can sell them at a profit. They're going to hope to sell them at the top and not have to sell them when the market takes a dive. They also forget that selling stock means there are taxes to pay, so even after holding something for twenty or more years, they receive the nasty surprise of owing a chunk of the gain to their silent partner: Uncle Sam.

So you have been introduced to one of the compounders available when you invest in the stock market, but there is another one that is even more powerful. I call it being a stock market landlord, and it is a way to make money on the stock even if the stock price drops. What the wealthy do is become a stock market landlord, and I'll show you how to join them in the next chapter.

Chapter 11
How to Become a Stock Market Landlord

Erik and Sara were aspiring real estate investors. Erik lived in Los Angeles, and Sara lived in Indianapolis, but they had both watched the same late-night infomercial where a guru was talking about buying properties for nothing down. They thought it sounded too good to be true but decided to see what it was all about. Both of them called in to order the package being advertised. Erik's package arrived but was missing the half of the workbooks. The second half was all on rental real estate, and since Erik was way more interested in making money on hot markets, he didn't care. Sara's package arrived but was missing the part of the series on hot markets. She only received materials on rental real estate.

Several weeks later, after spending some time watching the program and reading how it worked, they both started trying to obtain their first deal. To their surprise, the program actually worked and they both were able to obtain properties. They were both pretty excited because they knew that the wealthy always had real estate in their portfolios, and they knew that this was a key to wealth. However, Erik was all about the next hot market and Sara was more concerned with cash flow. As a result, Erik purchased a home in Los Angeles for $500,000, while Sara purchased a home in Indianapolis for $75,000. Both managed to get the owner to carry a loan for nothing down at a decent interest rate. Erik thought that because the market in Los Angeles was so hot, he would hold his property and the value would increase. Sara was not worried about the house she purchased increasing in value and instead concentrated on getting a tenant and rented the house for $800.

Erik was correct about the Los Angeles market, and his house increased in value by $50,0000 in the first year. The problem for Erik, however, was that he was bleeding cash on the loan—over $35,000 per year in principal and interest alone. Sara also had her loan payment, but it was less than $5,000 per year, and her rents easily covered that amount and put extra money in her pocket each month.

Erik was convinced that his property was going to continue to increase, so he held on. Because she had money coming in, Sara used it to buy additional properties, each one creating additional cash. The markets would sometimes fluctuate in Los Angeles but kept going up. Erik held on for ten years, and the house he purchased for $500,000 was now worth $750,000—a 50 percent increase. On the other hand, Sara had amassed ten houses at this point, at an average value of $100,000 each. She also had cash flow coming in each month of over $4,000.

One day Erik was talking to a savvy investor and telling him how well he had done on the home he purchased. How it had gone up 50 percent and he was cashing out. The savvy investor asked Erik, "Why didn't you rent the house out to someone else?" Erik looked at him blankly. Erik remembered that the guru's package he purchased all of those years back was missing half of the materials and wondered if that was what it had been missing. The savvy investor commented, "It was a great return, Erik, but you left an awful lot of money on the table by not renting out your property."

RENT YOUR STOCKS

In the last chapter, you learned where the wealthiest people invest. Now you're going to learn how to double up what you're earning out of those investments. So many casual investors don't know this information, but after you read this, you won't be one of them. Welcome to "How to Become a Stock Market Landlord." This is where we're really going to get into the fun part of this strategy.

We've studied how investing in the right stocks can give you a good dividend with a high return. Most investors in the stock market are like Erik from our story and are looking for the next hot market. They make their money gambling on the market going up. You should know by now that that is not the way to generate consistent and predictable wealth. We want excellent value, safety, and consistent payments of dividends. So now let's take it to the next level.

Wealthy investors buy good stocks and hold them. They collect their dividends on the stocks that they own, and then they also do something that might sound unusual—they *rent* their stocks. This is just like a owning a rental property, like what Sara did in the story. Some of you might have experience with rental properties, and in some ways stocks mirror the same principles. If you have a rental property, you don't want it to sit vacant. It's the same thing with the stock market. Yet so many people who own stocks just let them sit empty and unrented. Why is this?

To many people the stock market feels inaccessible. They quickly become overwhelmed with the data and the overload of investing advice that is out there. It is easy to become overwhelmed and paralyzed by the stock market. What I'm going to do in this chapter is break it down into smaller steps for you. And again, we're going to do what the wealthy do.

Let's consider, as an example, what happened with Microsoft. In 2000 Microsoft was trading at around seventy-six dollars. They were an expensive stock at the time, and a nice, upward-moving company. But then the market crashed in 2001, and Microsoft dropped to around twenty-two dollars. When the rest of the markets came back to the level at which they had been in 2000, Microsoft did not. This is what we call in the stock market world a *lagging stock*. They just floundered. They just couldn't get it together. It was not until seventeen years later that Microsoft came back to the seventy-six-dollar level. That's a massively long amount of time. Then it took off again, but there was the seventeen years of lost use of funds—lost opportunities, lost revenue. But not everyone felt the same pain.

Let's follow this through, because I want to show you how well this works for the wealthy investor and how others can get hurt. If you are a typical investor who owned Microsoft during this time, you're waiting for the stock to recover. You're either deciding to sell Microsoft and just dump it to be done with it, or you wait for seventeen long years for that stock to come back to where it was when you bought it. Since recovering, Microsoft has done really well, trading in the two-hundred-dollar range. But that was a long time to wait. And like I said, a lot of traditional investors just got bored with the stock and gave up on it. They were seeing no indication that it would ever come back to the levels that it was at in 2000. They sold at a loss and moved on. But when they did that, they missed the whole point of buying that stock. That is because they were using a traditional investor's mindset and not doing what the wealthy do. So let's examine the strategy of the wealthy investor.

Microsoft didn't pay a dividend at first or through the tech bubble, but they do now, and they have for years. The dividend right now is around two dollars, but this can change. They'll increase and sometimes decrease, but rarely do they decrease by much unless the company is having trouble. I'm going to give you the following numbers as a way to get to know this strategy.

If you own a hundred shares of Microsoft at $76 per share, you have $7,600 worth of value in that stock. Your dividend would have been $150 per year. Hopefully you're using that DRIP mentioned earlier and reinvesting the dividend payment back into purchasing more shares of stock. I know that $150 for an entire year doesn't sound that exciting, but if you just look at that one number, it doesn't mean a lot until you start to see the leverage. Hopefully I've built a pretty good case in the previous chapter showing you how valuable those dividends are. So while $150 per year might not sound too exciting by itself, what if you could take that and then increase it even more?

EVERY RENTAL NEEDS A LANDLORD

That brings us to this idea I have mentioned about renting out your stock and becoming a stock market landlord. With stock rental we have a great batch of opportunities to increase our cash flow, in a mode similar to Sara's rental portfolio. Think about it like this: when you rent property in the housing market, you're usually bringing in a monthly rent check. You can do the same thing in the stock market and receive monthly income and monthly rent checks, sometimes even weekly checks. Let's stick with Microsoft stock rental as the example.

Microsoft can be rented for about twenty to fifty cents per week. There are fifty-two weeks in a year. I don't want to overestimate this example, so I'm not going to assume that we're going to rent it every single week for fifty cents. So, let's average our rental right in the middle and say thirty-five cents per week of average weekly rental for Microsoft. Getting a weekly rental of about thirty-five cents is very doable on Microsoft. And as you can see, sometimes it may be a little bit less, but sometimes it's going to be a little bit more. I want to run the numbers conservatively so I will project that we will only rent half of the time, that's twenty-six weeks. When you learn how to use this strategy, you'll likely be able to rent more often and even bring in more money.

I want to make sure that we get the basics down and you get a really good feel for what the strategy is and how it works. Let's continue with the example that we own 100 shares of Microsoft. You're going to rent it for 26 weeks out of the year for $0.35, which means you're going to bring in $35 for every week that you rent this stock. If you do this for 26 weeks, that's $910 of rental income for that year. Not too bad. Remember that you also get the dividend of $150 per year. Even if you weren't so excited about this dividend originally, now you've just jumped it up considerably by renting the stock. And remember, you estimated conservatively that you would only be able to rent it for half of the year. The total return with your rental income of $910 and your dividend of $150 sums to over $1,000 for that year. Keep in mind this would have been over the course of seventeen years. Over that seventeen-year period of time that Microsoft stock did nothing, many investors sold their stock. If they had known how to be a stock market landlord, they could have leveraged their stock using it as a cash-flow vehicle and earned over $18,000.

To top it off, they would still own that stock today at a much higher stock price after the massive increase in share value. It gets pretty powerful when you see what you can do if you quit worrying about trying to time the sale of your stock and you turn your focus instead toward buying good stock and turning it into a cash-flow vehicle. And remember, that $18,000 profit just for renting that stock was based on a conservative estimate of renting the stock for only half of the year. What if you rented three-quarters of the year? You're bringing in more money already. And we ran these numbers for one hundred shares of stock. What if you had a thousand shares? Ten thousand shares? It just compounds and grows.

I ran the numbers on just one hundred shares of stock, but if you continued to receive your dividend, that dividend would be reinvested into more shares. As a result your leverage would actually be even higher than this. You would've made well over $18,000 in that seventeen-year period. In addition, you got those earnings and are still holding on to a great stock.

I know what you are thinking now: "Why aren't more people doing this?" Remember the story of Erik and Sara? Most people only get half of the materials and only half of the money. They are so focused on hot stock and appreciation that they either do not know about cash-flow options or they forget in all of their excitement. But as in Sara's story, the real secret is in allowing your money to compound, using the cash flow to increase your investments. By never being forced to sell anything, you do not take losses. By buying dividend stock, you have cash flow. By renting your stocks, you can multiply your cash flow considerably and you rent your stock by *selling options*.

THE OPTIONS MARKET

How do you actually rent a stock? Renting sounds straightforward in the world of real estate, but how do you do it in the stock market? The answer? It's all about the *options market*. It's actually a separate market that can present us with a number of different stock market advantages. We're going use the options market to rent our stock out, and we're going to be able to bring in cash flow way above and beyond the dividend payment that we're receiving. And then that dividend will be there to be that hedge for inflation and to continue to leverage out and help us accumulate more shares of stock.

Options are a contract between you and the market maker. If you're wondering who the market maker is, that's the person on the other side of your trade. This is why you can always buy and sell things in the stock market—because there's somebody there. Sometimes it's a real person, sometimes it's electronic, but there's a system or a person or something in place that will allow you to trade and always buy or sell. In the options market, someone is buying or selling a contract for the right to buy or sell a particular stock. For example, I might sell the market maker the right to buy 100 Microsoft shares at $2,250 each (known as the "strike price") for a period of 4 weeks for $1.00 per share. I would receive $100 in exchange for the obligation to sell. For the next 4 weeks, the market maker can force me to sell my Microsoft shares for $225 each, no matter what Microsoft is trading at. If Microsoft is at $230 per share, the market maker can still make you sell at $225. This is an option contract.

I suggest you focus on being the seller of options and avoid starting off as a buyer. There are plenty of option traders out there who love to buy options, but that is inappropriate for anyone starting out. I personally think options traders are professional gamblers. I live in Las Vegas and know the averages when gambling. Successful gamblers are in the single digits, and I believe successful option traders are about the same. Less than 10 percent will make money. On the flip side, 90 percent of the casinos (if not more) do make money. I think I would rather be the casino, and in the option market, the seller of an option on a stock that the seller already owns is the casino.

CALLS AND PUTS

Options always start with a contract. And there are two types of option contracts, *calls* and *puts*. The way this works is when you *buy* an option, you have certain rights, and when you sell an option, you have certain obligations. You have calls and puts, and you can either buy those or sell those. Let's go through the buying first.

You can buy a call option. It gives you the right to buy one hundred shares of a certain stock at a certain price, known as the strike price. You can buy that stock for a specific agreed-upon price, the strike price, for a set period of time. You can also buy a put option. It gives you the right to sell one hundred shares of a stock at an agreed-upon price for a set period of time. I just wanted to mention buying, but we are sellers of options. We are the casino. For right now and for the purpose of understanding stock renting, we're going to be sellers. If we're selling a call option, that will create the obligation for you to deliver or sell a hundred shares of a specific stock, at an agreed-upon price and at a certain time.

I like using the house example because it makes sense to a lot of people. Let's say you are in the market to buy a house, and you find a $200,000 house that you like. You're pretty excited about it. You could enter into a contract with the seller. You may say, "Look, don't really have the cash right now, but how about I give you earnest money for this contract? I'll pay you two thousand dollars for the right to buy your house." You set the terms, and that $2,000 gives you the right to buy the house for $200,000 within a set period of time. There will be restrictions. You have the right to buy this house within, let's say, thirty days, and you paid $2,000 for that right. That's the contract that you entered into. The seller of that contract—or in this example, the homeowner—has certain obligations. That homeowner cannot sell the house to anyone else during the contract term. And he must deliver the house at the agreed-upon price. He can't sell it to you for $300,000. You agreed that the price would be $200,000. If you do not end up buying that house, then he keeps the $2,000. If he keeps that money from the contract, you are not obligated to buy the house.

You get to decide. But he gets to keep the cash if you don't buy the house. In the stock market, options will work in the same way, much like the earnest money down you would put down on a house. Think of that earnest money as a call option that's similar to the $2,000 contract on the house. What happens is a call buyer has the right to purchase the stock at a certain price. That's if you buy a call option. If you are the seller, you have the obligation to deliver the stock. If you're the one that's sold that call option, you have the obligation to deliver the stock, much like if you are the owner of that house. If you sell that contract, you have the obligation to deliver if they want to buy the house.

RENT FIRST

I would suggest that you start with investing first because one of the problems with traders is that we run into the same problem that traditional investors have. And that is we have to time our sale. What if you buy a call option and instead of going up, it crashes? Your call ends up dropping significantly, and you end up losing money. Instead of doing that, what if we buy a stock that we can rent? Instead of buying call options and letting them run and then sweating the timing of things, we could do what the wealthy investors do. Let's buy a stock that we can rent out. If we could do that and we could bring in a consistent revenue stream through those rent checks and the dividends, that could take you out of this boom-and-bust cycle. Otherwise we have the market rallying and dropping and rallying and dropping. Everybody's freaked out, and then they're really happy, and then they're freaked out again, and then they're happy again and trying to catch the swings and make money. What if you could rent out your stocks as a cash-flow vehicle and not have to worry about the swings?

Let's go deeper into this strategy because that rent check is actually an option that you are going to sell against the stock that you already own. Remember that contract? We know that a call option is a contract between you and the market maker. It gives the buyer of the call option the right to buy a stock for a set price on or before a certain expiration date. So that's the call buyer.

What you will need to own is an optionable stock. If you own an optionable stock, you can sell to somebody else the right to buy that stock from you at a strike price and within a set period of time. That is the sale of the call option. That's your rent check. Now you are obligated to deliver that stock if the buyer chooses to take your stock at the strike price. It's just like that $2,000 earnest money on a house. If the homeowner sells that contract to somebody and that person comes back and says, "Yes, I want this house," they have to sell. You're doing the same thing in the stock market, and because you own the stock, you are selling a *covered call*. This is what the wealthy have been doing for years to make money on their portfolios without having to sell the underlying stock.

Instead of just waiting for stock to go up to make money, you can make money by renting your stock and collecting dividends all along the way. This is what was happening through that seventeen-year period with our Microsoft example. You're collecting dividends, you're writing covered calls because you own that underlying stock, you're collecting that rent premium for seventeen years, and you still own a company that you like and that over the long haul will serve you well.

The great thing about this is that it doesn't matter if the stock goes up or if it goes down or sideways because you got your cash-flow vehicle. Earlier in the book I talked about rental properties and how you don't worry about the value of the rental property. You just make sure the cash flows. You make sure there's money coming in because over time the values increase, and that's great.

This is the covered call strategy, and it works like this: you're going to buy a stock, you're going to bring in a rent check on that stock or sell a call against it, and if the stock goes up, you end up selling your stock. If the stock goes sideways or drops, you keep your stock and then you have it to *write* a call another day (write is just a stock market expression that means sell.) That's how you really could have owned Microsoft for seventeen years and never sold in that period but continually brought in that rent check.

But options in the stock market are even more versatile than options and rentals in the real estate market because in the stock market, you can buy back your option. Since this is an overview, I am not going to dig deep into this concept other than to plant the seed that you can sell an option for $1.00 and buy it back for $0.50. If the option goes back to $1.00, sell it again. If it drops, you can buy it back. Plenty of investors in our mastermind group make consistent money on this simple strategy.

Here is an example. Assume you buy XYZ stock and you pay $12.00 for the stock and you decide you're okay selling the stock at $13.00. You could sell a call option at a strike price of $13.00 and the value of that call is $1.20. You sold the right to somebody to buy your stock from you at $13.00. They may or may not buy the stock from you, but regardless of what they do, you just made $1.20 on this transaction. That's the rent check.

If the stock goes up to $14.00, do you know what's going to happen? They're probably going to choose to buy the stock from you at $13.00 rather than pay the $14.00 market price for the stock. They'll probably call (buy) the stock away from you. Is that okay? It's spectacular. You ended up making a dollar on the stock because you bought it at $12.00. Remember, you don't sell it at $14.00, you sell it at $13.00, and you bought at $12.00. Now you're up $1.00 on the stock plus a $1.20 premium for selling the call. You've made money, and you're up $2.20 on this investment. You can always buy the stock back when it dips or buy back the options, but the principle is to sell calls on the stocks you own.

Now, there are a couple other ways that this can play out too. You have the same XYZ stock, the one you bought at $12.00. And let's say we sell at that same $13.00 call option. We bring in the same $1.20 credit, and the XYZ stock goes down to $11.00. What do you think happens? Nobody's going to want to buy this stock from you at $13.00 if they can buy it on the open market for $11.00. What happens here is if the stock is trading at $11.00, you're going to keep that stock. You're going to rent it another day, but you also got to keep that $1.20. You keep that premium that you got for selling the call, and you still keep the stock.

Just as if you were the buyer of that $2,000 option on the house, and you said, "Oh wait, I just lost my job. I can't buy the house." Fine, you walk away; you don't buy the house. The owner keeps the house. What if something happens and the person that bought this call option doesn't want to take your stock? In this scenario, nobody will take your stock for $13.00 because they can buy it on the open market for $11.00, so you own the stock. You can write a call another day and you keep that $1.20 premium. Now here's an interesting thing: Do you worry about the fact the stock has gone down $1.00? No, because you realize that stocks are going to go up and down. Make sure you have a good stock, and make sure you've written the right call.

THE COVERED CALL

Let's examine another example. There's one other thing that could happen because stocks only move one of three ways—they go up, they go down, or they go sideways. What if we bought this stock at $12.00, we sell the same $13.00 call, we bring in a $1.20 credit, and then the stock goes up just a little bit to $13.00? This is the same price that somebody could buy the stock for on the open market. In this situation, where the stock is at the same price that you sold, do you know happens? You may or may not be called out. It might be a fifty-fifty chance. Sometimes you are, and sometimes you're not. And it doesn't matter either way. If you're called out, great, you sold your stock for a dollar profit and you keep the $1.20 for writing the call. If you aren't called out, you still keep your $1.20 and you own the stock to write the call the next week. We are going to write or sell a call—the right to buy the stock at a certain price by a certain time—and it's going to be against a stock that we own, which is *covered*.

This is the *covered call* strategy. And because we're writers or sellers of this call, we have the obligation to sell the stock—within that time period, of course. You pick the time period and the price; you have to sell it at that certain price within that time period if the buyer chooses to take it. Let's go back to the house example one last time. You're the owner of the house, and you sold the $2,000 contract to somebody and that gave them the right to buy that house at $200,000. It works the same way in the stock market. When you own the stock, you can sell a call against that stock that you own.

You might be reluctant to consider this approach because you're worried you can't afford one hundred shares of a stock like Microsoft. That's not a problem because the great thing about this strategy is that you can use it with anything that has options. You don't have to buy Microsoft or some other pricey stock to begin with. You can use a variety of different vehicles that fit your budget. There are stocks in the low ten-dollar price range, the teens, twenties, fifties, hundreds on up. You have a wide range of choices.

ETFS AND REITS

There is another vehicle called *exchange-traded funds*, often called *ETFs*. This is a basket of stocks and has advantages over buying a mutual fund. Not only can you buy an ETF and do better than if you had invested in a mutual fund, but then you could also sell calls against it. You can do the same covered call strategy with the ETFs. You would be better off not paying all those fees in the mutual funds, and now you're leveraging even more by writing calls and collecting dividends.

Along the same lines, there's also something called a *REIT*, which is a *real estate investment trust*. These ETFs and REITs vary widely in price. This gives you some choices, and you can start this strategy either really big or really slow and small. It might make sense for you to start slow and small just to understand how the strategy works and get the mechanics down. If you're just starting out and thinking long-term, this is a great place to start.

Let's review some of the steps to a covered call just to make sure you're clear on this.

The first thing you need to do is open a brokerage account. The next step is to buy stocks in groups of one hundred. That way you can sell your option and bring in your rent check. Keep in mind that you are going to find dividend stocks that meet our seven criteria (I will explain this in much greater detail in the next chapter.) Two of the seven criteria include the dividend being high enough and the stock having an options market. Assuming the seven criteria have been met and you have accumulated one hundred shares, you can write the covered call option. You're going to *sell that call to open.* That's the lingo that you're going to use. You're going to check your option chain to find the best risk and reward kind of option to sell. What this means is you're balancing between bringing in a good rent check and also trying to lower your chances of actually selling the stock. So there's a real sweet spot in there to make sure that you're selling the option to get your best reward for the lowest risk. I recommend that you sell *out of the money* options. This simply means that you sell the option for more than you purchased the stock for.

The worst-case scenario for you is the stock jumps up and you sell it for a profit and keep the option money. You still made money. This is a pretty powerful strategy, and this is why the wealthy do this. Once you do this, you write your covered call, and then you wait. You collect your dividends along the way, and if you're not called out, of course, you sell a call again. If you are called out, you could do one of two things. You could rebuy that same stock or you could find a brand-new investment. Maybe you've been researching another stock that you like. If you end up selling one stock, now you have cash in your account to reinvest elsewhere.

If the stock against which you sold an option starts to fall, the value of the option will also fall. If you sold an option at one dollar per share, you could buy it back for twenty-five cents per share. You can both buy back the option at a price less than the one you paid (called *buy the call to close*) and sell the stock if you are concerned it will fall further. I generally do not like to sell. In fact, I joke that my holding period is forever. I buy something because I want it in my portfolio. The only way I would sell a stock is if its dividends were cut drastically or it had some sort of major event like a scandal, major lawsuit, or disruptive technology that made it obsolete such that it that harmed the company to the point I had doubts about it recovering. Otherwise, I would just keep it and let its dividends pay for itself. When you have dividends and options, the stock will literally pay for itself over time and lower your risk of loss to zero.

This is the stock market landlord strategy in a nutshell. The options market is absolutely phenomenal when you use it as a landlord. Just like Sara in our story, you quit worrying about the stock increasing in value and focus on the rents. Over time you will hardly remember (or care) what you paid for the stock.

Chapter 12
How to Increase Your Financial Class

We have covered so much ground in this book to help you on your way to Infinity Investing. Now we're going to put all of this to work. This chapter is going to show you how you can start moving up in the different classes and improve your financial situation. You know where the wealthiest folks invest, you know how to become a stock market landlord by selling options on your dividend-producing stock—you're going to double dip on the profits that way, and you're going to be making money. I always tell people not to look at the value of your account—instead look at what it is producing. If we had a ticker symbol above our house or rental properties showing their value in real time, it would drive us crazy. Don't do that to yourself with your other assets. Look at what they're producing.

HOW TO MOVE UP

Now we're going to teach you how to increase your financial class from serf to apprentice to knight to steward. What you're going to learn in this chapter are the immediate steps to take. You will discover specific actions, action items, the Infinity Allocation Model, and how to create a ninety-day plan. At the very end, I will describe how you can join a support group that will give you a ton of information and support.

You will have access to a great deal of research and rating systems on stocks and continuous education on a monthly basis. This includes market analysis, breakdowns of certain stocks and opportunities in another asset category—real estate. You will be able to consult with professional fiduciaries who can teach you proper allocation and how to trade. We have professional investors in everything from individual rental properties to apartments, storage units, mobile homes, manufactured homes, currency, futures, and ETFs, among others. There is an old saying, "Your net worth is your network," and in this case we want your network to be Infinity. To get there, we need concrete steps.

The first thing you want to do is to figure out what you have to invest. Review your spread and determine what you can pay into the allocation model I am going to set out in a moment. Let's use the Jones family from chapter 4 as our example. If you recall, they have $1,000 of spread, and they have $1,000 of fat, which means that if they really wanted to, they could put $2,000 a month into the allocation model.

Your situation may be different. You may have more, you may have less, but you're going to want to figure that out and identify the amount that you are willing to commit to. Sometimes it's a good idea to treat it like a bill that you're paying on a monthly basis because you're going to need to feed this for it to really grow. So set a number and do it monthly like it's a utility bill. I do not care if you put it on autopay, but make it automatic so it does not depend on your doing anything to hold it up. Our worst enemy is generally ourselves when it comes to financial planning.

If you are just getting started and have little money, you may want to *paper trade* when building up. Paper trading is a fancy way of trading an imaginary account with imaginary money but using the actual numbers in the market. Think or Swim has a paper trading platform that will allow you to trade a pretend account and see how you do and learn. Ultimately there is no replacement for the actual "doing" of any strategy and seeing the results.

THE INFINITY ALLOCATION MODEL

Our allocation model is based on something one of our Certified Financial Planners calls the Yale model. Yale University's endowment has been remarkably successful over the years, including growing from $1 billion in 1985 to over $29 billion in 2019. The designer, David Swenson, had a unique approach to portfolio management where he considered cash a negative and focused on perpetual income, tax-favored investments, wide diversification of asset classes, and alternative investments. Like me, he looked at much of the mutual fund industry skeptically because of the conflict between managers and the investor and the excessive fees that are commonly present in mutual funds.

What we have done is taken many of the concepts from the Yale model and reduced them to something any investor can implement. This is called the Infinity Allocation Model. This model is very simple and has proved to be very successful in growth. Assets are held in the following areas:

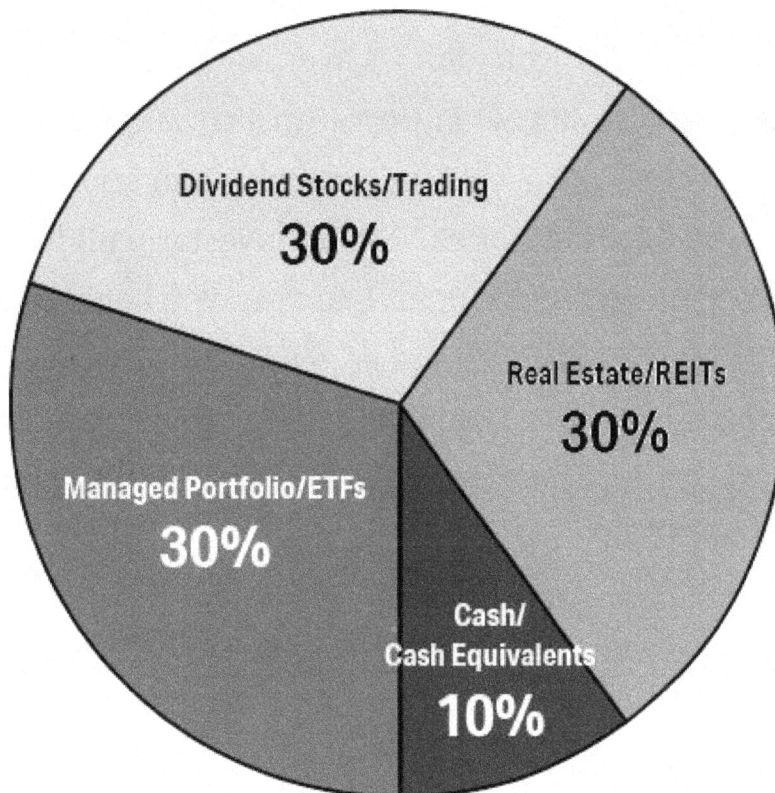

Number one is buying dividend stocks through your individual trading accounts. You're going to become a stock market landlord, just as you learned in chapter 11. Number two, you're going to be putting money into real estate. This doesn't mean just go out and buy a bunch of houses. I'm going to show you how you can invest in real estate through the stock market. There are opportunities there through publicly traded and private offerings. Number three is allocating 30 percent in a category called *managed portfolios*. This means that you are going to allow somebody else to oversee a very diverse portfolio. This might be managed ETFs or other kinds of funds, but not mutual funds. We are going to spend less than 1 percent on fees in a managed portfolio, but you're having somebody watching it 24-7 to make sure that you don't subject yourself to risk. You will see that in addition to the three investment categories, you will hold 10 percent in cash or cash equivalents for an emergency. More importantly, it will also be available for opportunities that arise. If you don't have the capital available when an opportunity arises, you're not going to be able to take advantage of it. We want to have that little safety net and opportunity fund set aside.

What if you're just getting started? For an investor with less than $50,000, we have an approach to get you started. Let's say you begin with $1,000. You would put $100 into cash and the other $900 into dividend stock. You're going to accumulate 100 shares, and you're going to keep doing this until you reach $50,000. At that point your $50,000 will be $45,000 in dividend-producing stock and $5,000 in cash.

SELECTING THE RIGHT STOCKS FOR YOUR PORTFOLIO

We're going to follow seven criteria to select the companies in which we will invest. In our Infinity online group, we use these seven criteria on stocks that have ten, twenty, twenty-five-plus, and fifty-plus years of consistent increases in dividends. I could write a book just on this subject alone, but I want to focus more widely on our Infinity Investing seven criteria for stock selection. These include:

- Price-charting

- Trend-charting

- Option-charting

- Dividend yield

- Revenue stability

- PE ratio

- Analysts

First, we always chart the stock price to make sure we are not buying something on a high. We do not want to be in the group that buys a stock right after it makes a new high. We want to buy a company after it comes off a high, hits a low, and is well on its way to coming back. To do this, we need to determine if the stock price has ever been at its current level in the past. Specifically, we want to see if the stock has surpassed or come within 5 percent of its current price within the past fifteen years. We don't want to buy it while it is on a high.

If you follow the markets at all, you're going to realize that there are trends and there are support lines, both upper prices and lower prices, that the stocks tend to bounce in between. These are called *support* (for lower) and *resistance* (for upper). You don't want to buy at the top. You want to buy after it's bottomed out and started to come back. You don't want to buy at the top or the bottom. Ideally you would buy somewhere closer to the bottom than the top, and at a price where the stock has been before. For example, if stock A is at $30, has it been at $30 before in the last fifteen years? If yes, what was its high during that period? What was the low? Let's say it has been at $42 in the past couple of years and is working its way up from a recent low of $25. If it is $30 today, it is $5 higher than its low and $12 below its high. This means it meets these criteria.

Second, we're going to see if it is trending up, down, or sideways (called a *channel*). Is it just kind of going sideways, or is it starting to go up? We do not want to buy a company on its downward trend. They call this "catching a falling knife." You want to make sure that the stock is either channeling or trending up.

You can determine the trend for any given period of time by drawing a straight line that hits all of the lows and highs on a chart. You would look at the lines to determine if the stock is trending up or sideways. If it is trending down, you avoid it. See below for examples of charts:

Trending Up:

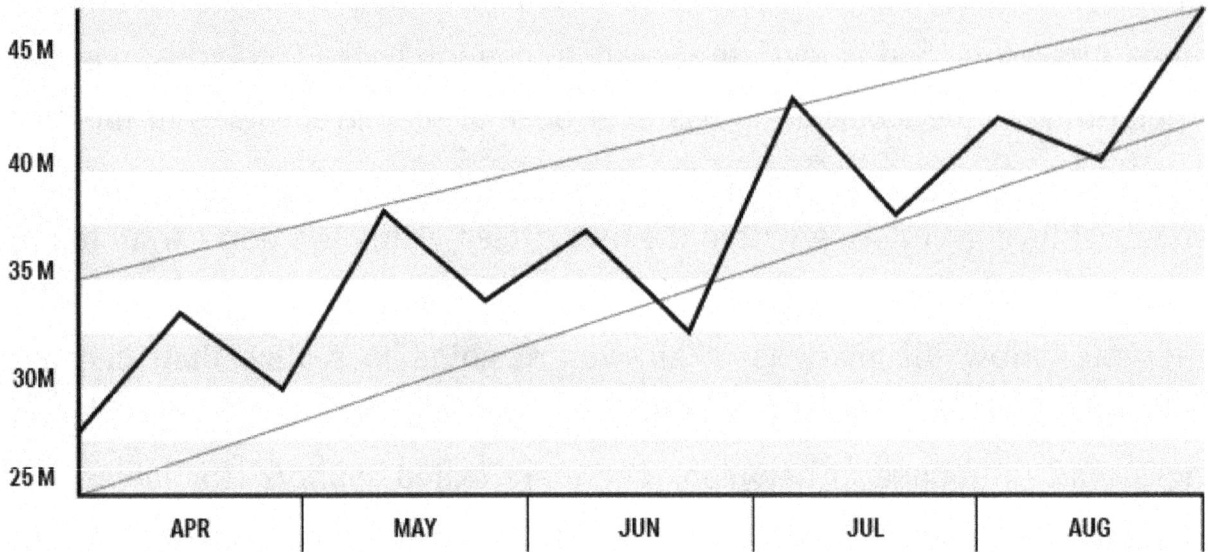

Channeling:

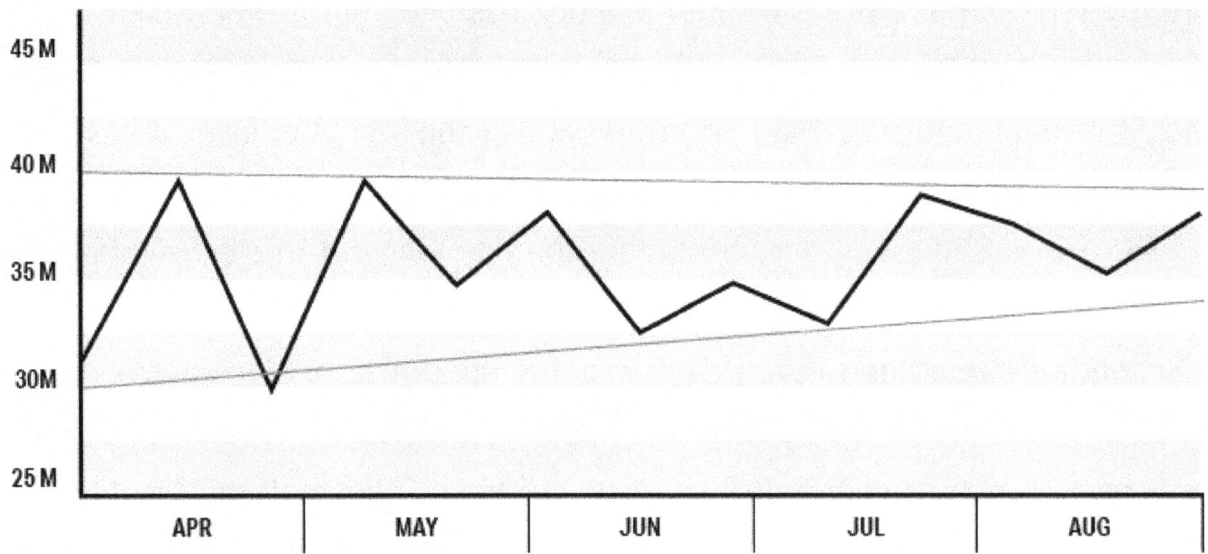

Trending Down:

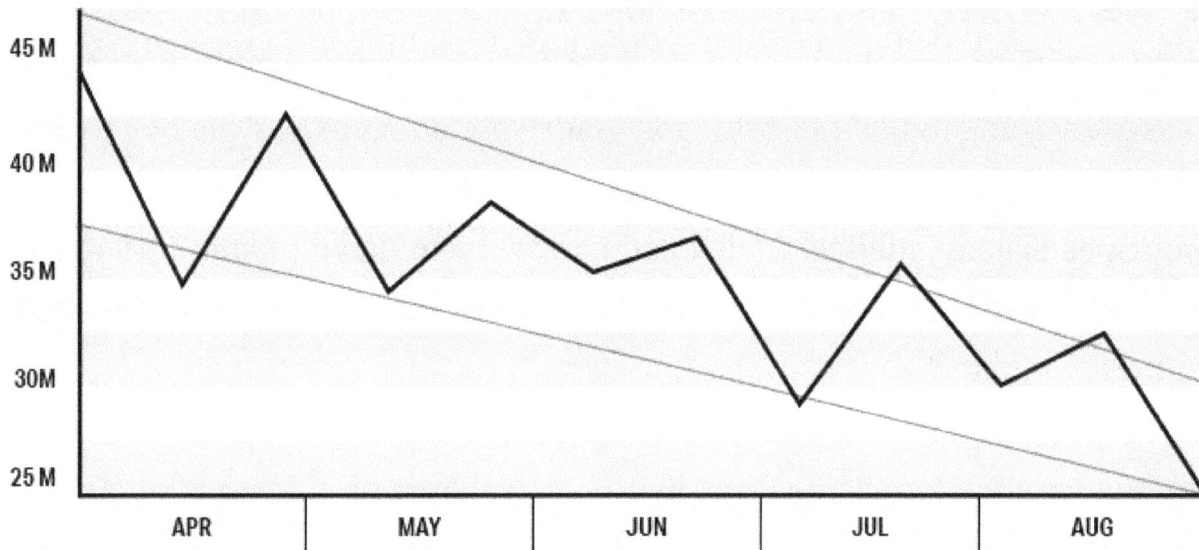

Third, does the stock offer option pricing? If so, is it weekly or monthly, and is it worthwhile? You can always tell if options are offered by looking at the option chains available in just about any major brokerage platform or by going to Yahoo! Finance (free) and clicking on "Options" after pulling up any stock quote.

Fourth, we determine if the yield has been consistent over the last five years. If so, does it consistently beat the 2 percent yield mark? The yield is available on any stock quote.

Fifth, we look to see if the stock has had stable revenue. Is this stock with a solid company that is continuing to prosper no matter what the economy is like? We do this by looking at the last three years to see if there have been big fluctuations in the stock price. A stable stock is one whose fluctuations are within 10 percent. The exception could be if the fluctuation was higher due to nonrecurring one-time events like the COVID-19 pandemic. You will want to look at the *top line* revenue, also known as the *total revenue,* to ensure the company has not fluctuated downward more than 10 percent in the last three years.

Sixth, examine the *price to earnings ratio,* also known as the *PE ratio.* You want it to be somewhere between fifteen and twenty-five—but whatever the case, less than twenty-five. We don't want it to be hurting. We want it to be right in that sweet spot of solid companies that are not getting shaken out. You're not going to buy the risky and you're not going to buy the overpriced. You're going to buy right in your sweet spot. This will take the thousands of companies that are publicly traded and narrow them down to about fifty. This will likely have a *TTM* (trailing twelve months) next to it. This represents the last twelve months.

The PE ratio is simple math. You take the stock price as quoted and divide it by the earning per share (EPS) that is also shown on the stock quote. If a company is twenty-five dollars per share and its earnings are one dollar per share, the PE ratio is twenty-five.

Seventh, you're going to review analysts' reports to determine if anybody has a strong opinion. You're going to ignore the holds. We're only going to look at recommendations of buy or strong buy versus underperform or sell. And we need to see a ratio of at least three positive comments, or analysts, to every negative one.

This is critical and will help you keep from making mistakes. You want to get seven out of seven of these metrics before you buy that stock. It doesn't mean that there's ever a guarantee, but what it means is that stock is strong and it's much less likely that you're going to have a bad experience with that company.

Remember that you want to focus on the dividend aristocrats and dividend kings. The aristocrats are the companies that have been paying out increasing dividends for twenty-five years, and the kings are the companies that have been paying out increasing dividends for fifty years. It's very difficult to kill off those companies. They are fighters. These are the Coca-Colas of the world, the 3Ms. These are the Johnson & Johnsons, the Proctor & Gambles, even the Tootsie Rolls. These are really big, sometimes boring, companies.

That said, it is possible that the company does some really dumb things, in which case you're going to want to bail out of them. You will know way ahead of time when they start to drop, but it is rare.

Then after you accumulate one hundred shares, you're going to write options on those one hundred shares. You will be selling an *out of the money* option. You can't lose because you are going to agree to sell it at a price that's greater than what you bought it for. Let's go back to the Infinity Allocation Model I showed you at the beginning of the chapter. The idea is that you are going to invest $50,000 in that category, then you are going to move to the next category.

THE $50,000 PORTFOLIO

Infinity Allocation Model for First $50,000:

Dividend Stock: $45,000

Cash: $5,000

From that first $50,000, you are going to invest $45,000 in stock—specifically, stocks that meet seven out of seven criteria. Five thousand dollars is going to be in cash or cash equivalents. Money markets, savings, CDs, precious metals are all cash equivalents. Whatever you're holding in the stock market, you could turn that into cash in two days as well, so it is also easy to liquidate. You can get that cash in an emergency very quickly if you ever need to. You're investing in really boring companies that don't fluctuate much because you don't want to be in a situation where the stock dropped 30 percent and now you have to sell to pay some unexpected bills. That is a horrific situation to be in. Just ask anyone who lived through a market crash and had to sell their stock in a drastically down market to pay their bills. You cannot call the utility company and ask, "Can I pay my bill when the market recovers?" They just turn off your lights. Even when the market tanked 38 percent in 2008, the dividend kings only went down a total of 14 percent. We want to do whatever we can to avoid major swings.

BEYOND $50,000

Infinity Allocation Model for First $100,000:

    Dividend Stock: $45,000

    Real Estate: $45,000

    Cash: $10,000

When you get past that first $50,000, then you're going to start to allocate money to real estate. Don't assume this means going out and just buying rental property yourself (although that is fine). You can do this instead by buying shares in something called a *real estate investment trust*, or *REIT*. They're publicly traded and are just like stock, but they're real estate based and have to distribute a high percentage of their earnings to keep their REIT status. By their nature they are cash flow oriented.

You could even do something called *private placements*. These are private offerings that were traditionally only offered to the wealthiest investors, also known as *accredited investors*. The rules have been greatly reduced over the last years and more and more offerings are available to ordinary folks with rules imposed by the SEC and states to protect investors. I know some investors love multifamily real estate but do not want to risk all of their money on one project. They often pool their money with other investors to spread out the risk. That is a typical private placement, but they can be used for just about anything. In our allocation model, the types of investments should be real estate, including single family, multifamily, and mobile homes, RV parks, storage, or similar projects.

I started my real estate investing with single family residences. I suggest most others do the same, but by focusing on great deals at much lower price points than the gurus teach. First, there is always a market for single family homes. They are the American dream—a home of your own. We just pay close attention to the numbers that really matter. We stick to areas where there is low unemployment and lots of need. We also only invest if the deal is cash flow positive. If a house rents for $1,500 per month, that does not automatically make it a good deal. On the other hand, the fact that a house is renting for $500 per month does not make it a bad deal. What matters is how much we will get to keep each month and how much we will need to invest. A house that rents for $2,000 per month that is vacant 25 percent of the time will likely prove to be a money pit. By comparison, a house that rents for $1,000 per month but has an average tenancy of five years may prove to be a great deal. That may simply come down to how much it costs to fix the home in between tenants, how much taxes and insurance cost, and how much of the rent charged is actually collected.

When I look at homes, I calculate what the house could rent for on a monthly basis and cut it in half (if the house rents for $1,000 per month, I assume I will actually see $500 per month after expenses). I assume my expenses, including managers, insurance, taxes, repairs, improvements, vacancy rate, and other expected expenses, will eat up at least 50 percent of the gross rents received. Of the amount received, you still have to cover the mortgage payment, so there has to be more coming in than will be going out after paying all expenses, including debt service.

Let's take the example of buying a house at $120,000 that rents for $1,500. You might think this is a great deal by looking at it. Assume it brings in 50 percent of the gross rent, or $750, per month. That means its net income would by $9,000 per year. Not bad. If you were buying with cash, your return would be 7.5 percent plus any appreciation. In commercial real estate, this is called the *CAP* rate or *capitalization rate*. This number allows us to compare properties in almost any market by knowing what a good CAP rate is in that particular market. For our purposes, the CAP rate just tells us a starting point for return on our money. Note: Sneaky real estate agents will take your eye off the ball by talking about *comp rates* (comparable properties) and ignore the CAP rate. They might say, "A house just like yours sold down the street for fifty thousand dollars more than yours." Investors use CAP rates as their greatest factor because they are more interested in the return on their money than the appreciation. A great CAP rate always sells, while the values of comps fluctuate wildly, just like the stock market.

Now let's assume you financed the property, put nothing down, and the interest rate your bank offered was 5 percent. Your payment would be $645 per month, or $7,740 per year. You are still in positive territory, but barely. If you are interested in that property, you would sharpen your pencil and make sure you know all potential expenses associated with the property. If the actual expenses are 45 percent or lower, the answer is easy—buy it. Closer to 50 percent, you still might be willing to buy but notice how close you are from having an asset versus a liability. It is for that reason that I never recommend anyone go below 75 percent debt to equity in rental real estate unless there is an extraordinary CAP rate. By having $30,000 down on a $120,000 home, your payment drops to $484 per month. All of a sudden, you are in a much stronger position. Over time, the loan is paid off in full and you not only own the house outright but you also gain its appreciation and continuous cash flow.

We're not going to get rich quick or make gazillions of dollars, but we're going to make nice consistent returns day after day, week after week, month after month, and year after year. And it's going to grow. Then if you wanted to, you could buy single family residences, duplexes, or quads. I wouldn't jump right into multifamily. Cut your teeth on single family residences. And before you say, "Oh, fifty thousand dollars isn't going to get me much," there are communities where you could buy two houses for that. There are communities where you could buy a very good house for $50,000 that will produce a nice income stream.

Having said that, and averages being what they are, you're always better off with ten properties as opposed to one because if you have one property and one vacancy, you have a 100 percent vacancy rate. The numbers can get skewed for good or bad in a hurry, which kind of stinks. If you have one roof you have to fix, all of a sudden it's going to ruin your year. It's better to have multiple properties to even out the averages.

Also notice that the numbers do not work well with more expensive homes. Once you get up over $200,000 to $300,000 per home, it is exceedingly difficult to make consistent cash flow. CAP rates drop quickly, meaning these are not really investments; they are speculation. Speculation homes may have a place in someone's portfolio, but probably not for cash-flow investors. The sweet spot for rentals with cash-flow seems to be in the $75,000 to $150,000 area with slight variations depending on the deal. The people I know who stay in this range do well. The people who go way above that almost always end up subsidizing the properties with their own money. That is something we want to avoid.

BEYOND $100,000

What would your allocation model look after the first $100,000? Ten percent, or $10,000, is in cash, $45,000 is in dividend stock that you are renting out, and now $45,000 is sitting in real estate. After that we move to the next category, which is a managed portfolio. You can either hire your own money manager or mirror a managed portfolio. The managers I work with generally give you three different categories; conservative, moderate, and aggressive (for those who are willing to risk more to make more). They manage this portion of your portfolio for you. You will see what these portfolios look like, and you might be surprised that there are not a ton of different things in them. They are actually quite simple and usually heavy on ETFs. This means that the managers buy big chunks of a certain *sector* (lots of different companies in a bucket) with one share of an ETF. The ETF is managed almost like a mutual fund without all the downside and without all the added expense. The manager is selecting multiple ETFs to help spread risk, and the ETF manager is managing the ETF to reduce risk at the same time. This is a two-for-one where everyone is aligned. Your portfolio, regardless of size, can be managed just like an enormous portfolio, generally for less than 1 percent. Now you have somebody watching your money 24-7 without paying the massive price tag of a mutual fund (1 percent as compared to 5 percent).

Infinity Allocation Model for $150,000 and above:

> Dividend Stock: $45,000 (30%)
> Real Estate: $45,000 (30%)
> Managed: $45,000 (30%)
> Cash: $15,000 (10%)

When you get to that $150,000 number, you have 30 percent invested in the three categories and 10 percent in cash. If you are above $150,000, it works the same way. (We have folks that have tens of millions of dollars and they're still using this model, because it works.) Let's say someone had one million dollars in their 10 percent cash allocation. That doesn't mean they put it in a checking account. They may have it in a money market or other interest-bearing account. Some people will actually put it in the equities anyway. Additional stocks, maybe bonds, or something else that's easy to turn into cash.

Infinity Allocation Model for $1,000,000:

Dividend Stock: $300,000 (30%)

Real Estate: $300,000 (30%)

Managed: $300,000 (30%)

Cash: $100,000 (10%)

To keep the example simple, let's consider the Infinity Allocation Model for $1 million. They would have $100,000 in cash and $3000,000 each in dividend stocks, real estate, and managed funds.

By following these proportions, you can manage your portfolio responsibly no matter its size. You might be wondering what your immediate next steps are, and I will set that up for you in the next chapter.

Chapter 13
What to Do in the Next Ninety Days

Jimmy was one of the smartest people at his university. In fact, his GPA was 4.1, meaning he averaged over an A. He was valedictorian of his class as an economics major, and everyone knew he would go on to greatness. When he graduated, he was offered prestigious positions at other universities. He became an economics professor and was generally regarded as one of the best in his field. He earned his PhD and became the "go-to" professor to interview on news or other TV programs for his expertise. If there was a crisis or a big boom, the talking heads on TV wanted his opinion, and Jimmy enjoyed this role.

The only problem was that being a famous economics professor had pressures. He believed that he needed to live in the right neighborhood and drive the right car. This was costly. While his salary was great—he was in the top 5 percent of wages in the United States—he was still incurring debt to maintain his lifestyle. In his fifties, he realized that he was not much further along than when he graduated. He was genuinely worried about having to reduce his lifestyle when he retired, if he was going to be able to retire at all.

Several of Jimmy's students had become successful entrepreneurs, business owners, and executives. Many were financially independent and loved running things by their old professor. On one of these occasions, Jimmy turned things around and began asking questions of his student. On this occasion the student, Jennifer, had reached out for Jimmy's thoughts on the real estate market. There had been a major drop in the retail sector of real estate, and Jennifer was interested in what Jimmy thought. Jimmy crunched the numbers and realized that retail was going to have a rough go of it in the short term until new uses of the space were identified. Jennifer thanked the professor, but before she could go, Jimmy asked her, "I have been at the top of my field for a while now, yet I am not far ahead financially. What am I doing wrong, Jennifer?"

Jennifer was caught off guard and said, "Nothing. You are the best in your field."

But the professor knew better and pushed. "Come on, you must have more to say. What am I doing wrong?"

Jennifer looked at her old professor wryly and said, "Knowledge is knowing a tomato is a fruit, but wisdom is knowing that putting tomato in your fruit salad will ruin it." She then chuckled, but saw that the professor was not joining in. She became serious and explained, "There are plenty of really smart people out there with lots of knowledge, but without action that knowledge is wasted."

The professor responded, "I use my knowledge to help students such as yourself."

To which Jennifer said, "And I am sure you are paid well to teach, but the market determines what that is worth unless you choose to leverage your knowledge." Jimmy thought about this for a minute and asked her to clarify. "Professor, you can teach about one hundred students per year at your university, and the university charges them X dollars per credit hour, so your compensation is generally limited unless you leverage it. You can leverage it by publishing your works, by creating content, by syndicating your predictions, by licensing the formulas you have created, by investing in accordance with your knowledge, and any number of other ways. But you have chosen to use your labor as your primary source of income and have not planted the seeds of your knowledge in the market to allow them to yield fruit."

The professor caught on quickly and responded, "I have not been practicing what I preach?"

"Exactly," Jennifer stated.

That night Jimmy made a commitment to planting the seeds of his knowledge in various markets. Jennifer's words would not be lost on him, and even though he was one of the smartest people in academia, he had not been wise enough to allow himself to see the truth. He was only one man, and without leveraging his time and talents, he would never be truly free. He would always be exchanging his time for money unless he planted his seeds wisely. He laughed out loud when he thought about it: "What do you get if you eat the seeds for your harvest … a turd made of seed."

YOUR NEXT STEPS

Now let's talk about next steps for you. You are going to start planting seeds right away, and you are going to allow them to mature. You are going to replant the harvest until such time as you can live off the harvest. Until that time, you need to commit to keeping the seed, planting it, allowing it to harvest, and replanting the harvest. To do this, we need to determine exactly where you are in the allocation model. Once we do that, we can determine next steps. Determine what your allocation model is going to look like based off of your investable asset base.

Go to the level below that describes your investable asset base.

LEVEL ONE: IF YOU HAVE LESS THAN $50,000 IN INVESTMENTS AND CAPITAL, INVEST IN DIVIDEND

STOCKS

With your income spread, you're just going to start off by buying shares of dividend-producing stocks. You're going to find the seven-out-of-sevens, and you're going to invest in one of those until you reach one hundred shares. Just use Robinhood or some other fee-free option so that you're not paying any transaction fees. One hundred percent of your money is going straight to the stock. Do not forget to follow our allocation model and put aside one dollar in cash for every nine dollars you invest in stock. Put that cash in a savings account, market account, or something along those lines. You could even buy a bond ETF, something that's very low risk so that you're not going to worry about fluctuations in the market.

Once you hit one hundred shares, you are going to do two things. First, you are going to sell an option on the one hundred shares you purchased. This will be an *out of the money* option for whatever your average purchase price of your shares was. If you purchased one hundred shares of PG between $97 and $101 per share, you would determine your average price paid. You will see this as your total *stock basis* (total amount you paid) divided by one hundred. If your average share price was $99, you would only sell calls at a strike price at above $99.

Second, you are going to identify another seven-out-of-seven stock and start the process over again. Keep doing this until you are close to the $50,000 mark of total stock value and cash. Then you progress to level two—steps for assets over $50,000 but less than $100,000.

LEVEL 2: IF YOU HAVE MORE THAN $50,000 BUT LESS THAN $100,000 IN INVESTMENTS AND CAPITAL

Step One. Invest in Dividend Stocks

You're going to start off by just allocating $45,000 for buying shares of dividend-producing stocks. You're going to find the seven-out-of-sevens, and you're going to invest in one hundred shares of each stock until you have invested $45,000. Remember to use the fee-free option and to put aside one dollar in cash for every nine dollars you invest in stock.

Put that cash in a savings account, market account, or something along those lines. You could even buy a bond ETF, something that's very low risk so that you're not going to worry about fluctuations in the market.

Next you are going to sell options on each of the one hundred shares you purchased. This will be an *out of the money* option for whatever your average purchase price of your shares was. If you purchased one hundred shares of PG between $97 and $101 per share, you would determine your average price paid. You will see this as your total stock basis divided by one hundred. If your average share price was $99, you would only sell calls at a strike price at above $99.

Second, you are going to research REITs and other real estate opportunities with the amount of money you have in excess of $50,000. (Again, remember to allocate one dollar for every nine dollars into cash.) You will want to identify at least two real estate opportunities to compare and contrast. They might be a rental properties and a REIT, two REITs, or a REIT and a private placement. So long as it is real estate, it does not matter. You just want to get in the habit of giving yourself options so you can spot a good deal in the future and in order to help shorten the learning curve. Once you identify your opportunities, go to step two.

Step Two. Invest in One Opportunity

Compare and contrast your opportunities and choose the investment you are most comfortable with first. Now invest.

This is the most fun step, investing in real estate. If you invest in a REIT, it feels about the same as buying a stock, but it will open your ears to new terminology and a world where REITs are forced to pay out profits. If you invest in individual real estate investments, you will learn what it means to be a landlord and will quickly develop a whole new understanding of what is important and what is hype. If you chose a private placement, watch and listen closely to what the project management says and does. They have a duty to you, and you can learn a lot by watching and listening to professionals and what metrics they focus on and how they invest. Whatever the case, you learn by doing, so try to be involved in this step as much as you can. When you speak to other real estate investors, you will start to hear things that you missed before and you will develop a new vocabulary. Depending on what type of investments you do, you will start to develop an expertise that only comes from experience in that type of real estate.

If you have additional funds to invest, repeat step two until you reach $100,000 in investments, then go to the steps for assets over $100,000 but less than $150,000.

LEVEL THREE: IF YOU HAVE MORE THAN $100,000 BUT LESS THAN $150,000 IN INVESTMENTS AND CAPITAL (GO TO LEVEL TWO AND COMPLETE STEPS ONE AND TWO. THEN GO TO STEP THREE BELOW)

Step Three. Managed Money

For whatever amount of money you have in excess of $100,000 but less than $150,000, you are going to either hire a money manager or mirror a managed portfolio. I recommend that you find a fiduciary to manage your money for a set fee. They generally charge a percentage of assets under management and will work with you to determine your risk tolerance and goals. I am partial to fiduciaries because they are legally required to put your interests before their own. Remember Bob the butcher? Good guy, competent butcher, *not* a fiduciary.

Our goal for this portion of our investments is to have the input of professional third parties to continue our learning and to expand our thinking. Of course it is to make money as well, but what we are really looking for is someone who will care for our money 24-7 so we can learn what they are doing. That is not to say we are spying on them for nefarious reasons. It is quite the opposite. They are working for you, so you should get the most benefit you can from the relationship. Because they are a professional, you will necessarily learn things from them that you can utilize to become a better investor.

If you cannot meet a minimum requirement to open an account with your preferred money manager, then mirror an account allocation from another. This just means you pay to have a CFP or fiduciary create an allocation model for you (something most will do). Alternatively, you could find one online (some are available via subscription), and you follow it until you have enough to transition to full-time management. These portfolios are usually heavy in ETFs, so mirroring is not really that difficult. As you already know, ETFs are also managed. They change slowly because there is a lot of thought behind what is included in the ETF, so do not expect whiplash from all of the trades.

Again, my preference is to hire a fiduciary and to start a long-term relationship. Our mastermind group has several whom we work with. As a result, you can always find one who follows the Infinity model by joining our mastermind. Our group does not handle investments, and we do not own an advisory firm, so we have no dog in the fight for whomever you chose. As long as they are open and honest and grasp the Infinity concept, just about any fiduciary can help. You are looking for people who are willing to teach you along the way, so just make sure anyone you speak to understands and accepts that role when you engage them.

Once you hit $150,000, then the model is simple: 10 percent in cash, 30 percent in dividend stock, 30 percent in real estate, and 30 percent in managed money. Reevaluate your portfolio no less than annually and not more often than quarterly and make sure you are allocating correctly.

LEVEL FOUR: IF YOU HAVE $150,000 OR MORE IN INVESTMENTS AND CAPITAL

Do not go to any of the previous levels, as your investments will be based on a percentage of total investments and capital.

Step 1. Invest in Dividend Stocks

Start off by allocating 30 percent of your investable capital into buying shares of dividend-producing stocks. You're going to find the seven-out-of-sevens, and you're going to invest in increments of one hundred shares of each stock. If you have a sizable portfolio (over $100,000 in capital), this might take some time, as you do not want all of your eggs in one basket. I would suggest you buy no fewer than five different companies and divide your buying evenly until you have completely allocated your investments.

You are going to sell options on the shares you purchased. These will be *out of the money* options for whatever the average purchase price of your shares was.

Step 2. Invest in Real Estate

Allocate 30 percent of your investable capital into buying real estate assets.

Research REITs and other real estate opportunities with the amount of money you have allocated. You will want to identify at least two real estate opportunities to compare and contrast. They might be a rental property and a REIT, two REITs, or a REIT and a private placement. So long as it is real estate, it does not matter. You just want to get in the habit of giving yourself options so you can spot a good deal in the future and shorten the learning curve. Compare and contrast your opportunities, and choose the investment you are most comfortable with first. Now invest.

If you invest in a REIT, it feels about the same as buying a stock, but it will open your ears to new terminology in a world where REITs are forced to pay out profits. If you invest in individual real estate investments, you will learn what it means to be a landlord and will quickly develop a whole new understanding of what is important and what is hype. If you choose a private placement, watch and listen closely to what the project management says and does. They have a duty to you, and you can learn a lot by watching and listening to professionals and what metrics they focus on and how they invest. Whatever the case, you learn by doing, so try to be involved in this step as much as you can. When you speak to other real estate investors, you will start to hear things that you missed before and you will develop a new vocabulary. Depending on what type of investments you do, you will start to develop an expertise that only comes from experience in that type of real estate.

If you have additional funds to invest, repeat step two until you have invested the 30 percent of the total. Be slow and steady, and consider each transaction separately.

Step 3. Managed Money

For the 30 percent allocated to managed money, you are going to hire a money manager. I recommend that you find a fiduciary to manage your money for a set fee. They generally charge a percentage of assets under management and will work with you to determine your risk tolerance and goals. I am partial to fiduciaries because they are legally required to put your interests before their own. Remember Bob the butcher? Good guy, competent butcher, *not* a fiduciary.

Our goal for this portion of our investments is to have the input of professional third parties to continue our learning and to expand our thinking. Of course it is to make money as well, but what we are really looking for is someone who will care for our money 24-7 so we can learn what they are doing. That is not to say we are spying on them for nefarious reasons. It is quite the opposite. They are working for you, so you should get the most benefit you can from the relationship. Because they are a professional, you will necessarily learn things from them that you can utilize to become a better investor.

Again, my preference is to hire a fiduciary and to start a long-term relationship. Our mastermind group has several whom we work with. As a result, you can always find one who follows the Infinity model by joining our mastermind. Our group does not handle investments, and we do not own an advisory firm, so we have no dog in the fight for whomever you chose. As long as they are open and honest and grasp the Infinity concept, just about any fiduciary can help. You are looking for people who are willing to teach you along the way, so just make sure anyone you speak to understands and accepts that role when you engage them.

Do not forget to keep 10 percent of your investments in cash or cash equivalents. We always want dry powder for opportunities that come along, as well as an emergency fund. There is nothing worse than having to liquidate a portfolio in a down market, so having this cash is essential to our financial well-being.

Follow the rules: 10 percent in cash, 30 percent in dividend stock, 30 percent in real estate, and 30 percent in managed money. Reevaluate your portfolio no less often than annually and not more often than quarterly. Over time you will find this model is far superior and easier to follow than just about anything out there.

FINAL THOUGHTS

By now you should have a pretty good grasp of what Infinity Investing is all about. This is not a get rich program by any stretch. It is about getting rich slowly and methodically using time-tested strategies. I know the strategies work because I see the tax returns of thousands upon thousands of investors and I see the hard evidence of who makes money and who loses. The IRS also publishes a ton of data each year in its annual Data Book that is a treasure trove of information. Lastly, the Federal Reserve, through its Federal Reserve economic data (FRED), gives us enough historical data to see exactly what investments in different types of assets have done over the decades to help guide us in our decisions. Armed with this information, an Infinity Investor can start down the path of building a cash-flow machine that will withstand the test of time.

What every Infinity Investor will need to grapple with is the fear of losing out on the short-term roulette that plays out daily in the stock market and in the "hot" real estate markets. An Infinity Investor will not gamble his or her future on a Tesla or Amazon, so they might miss out on some of the larger short-term gains. At the same time, they are also avoiding the devastation of owning Napster and Infospace—two of many companies caught in the tech bubble bust of 2000. Trust me, there will be more as companies exceed reasonable valuations and have share prices based on hype and potential for the future.

That is not to say you should not and cannot buy speculative stocks or invest in upstarts with great potential. Such investments should be treated like "gambling money" or, put another way, money you can afford to lose. You do not bet your rent money on horse races, and similarly Grandma should not bet her living money on speculative stocks, no matter how much of a "sure thing" they seem. Instead, the Infinity Investor builds a beast of a cash-flow machine. A machine that can handle major fluctuations in the economy and still consistently kick off cash.

While the Infinity Investor should invest with the mindset that they are buying assets for an infinite period of time, meaning our holding period is forever, they should also know that when an asset's income stream is compromised, it is time to trade it in. Think of it this way: if you have an ice maker in your refrigerator and it stops making ice, replace it. If you have a cash-flow asset that stops producing cash flow, replace it. It is no longer an asset if it is not producing, so it is time to sell it or trade it for something that produces.

Infinity Investors have the luxury of being somewhat lazy. While we like to sell options on our stocks, for example, we also know that we can do that in thirty minutes per month. While we love cash flow from real estate, we also know that we can determine the rate of return for any given property in a matter of minutes. Being an Infinity Investor is not time-consuming. That said, it has been proven that to develop any good skill set (called the learning curve), it takes approximately twenty hours to get really good at it. If you want to be an expert at something, it might take ten thousand hours, but that is because the learning curve looks like this:

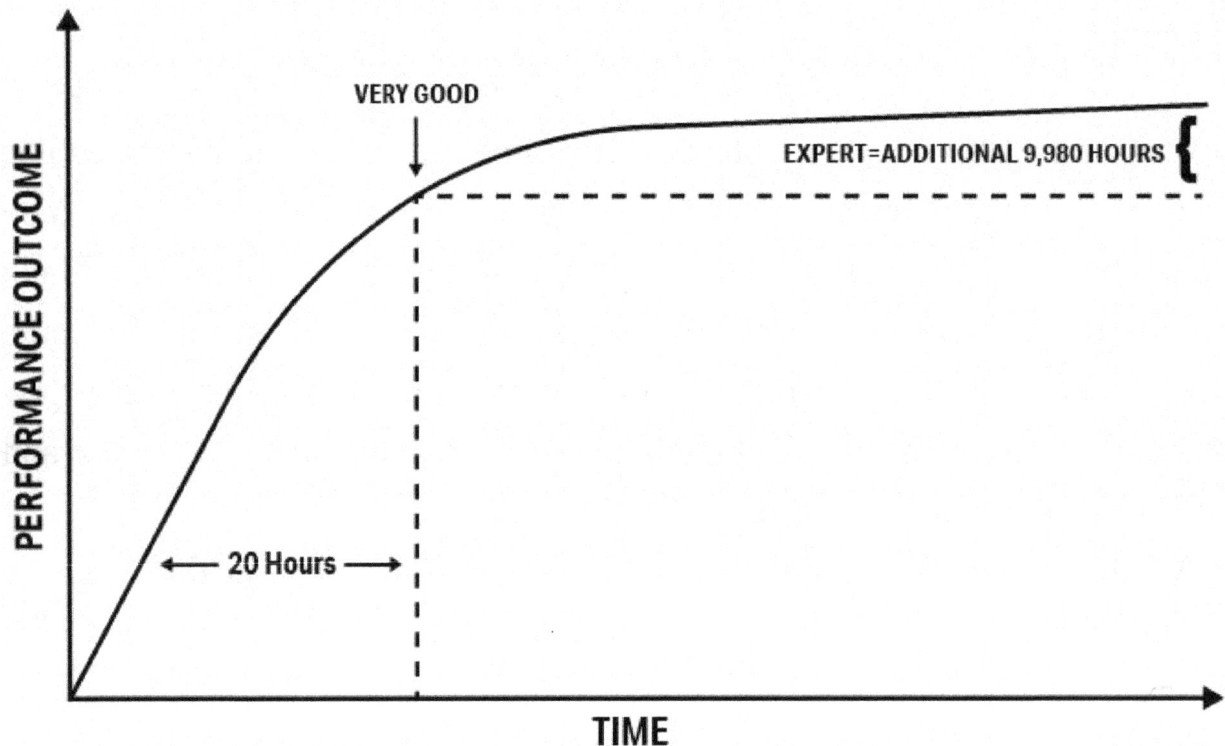

New Infinity Investors are closer than they realize to getting very good at the system. Just reading this book has launched your progress. Our free resources, including the Infinity Investing Workshop, will cover much of the rest. For those of you who want to implement the system and build your own cash-flow machine to reach Infinity, there are ample resources and opportunities to implement at **InfinityInvestingWorkshop.com**.

Welcome to the world of Infinity Investing.

ACKNOWLEDGMENTS

This book is a culmination of experiences put into writing. They are not just my experiences, but the experiences of the tens of thousands of investors I have had the opportunity to teach, the tax returns and financial data of so many successful investors that I have had the opportunity to review, and the experiences of fellow teachers. Many of the strategies herein were designed in conjunction with some fantastic investors who have achieved amazing results. For example, when I write about the stock market landlord, I rely heavily on Markay Latimer, a friend and investor, whom I knew in 1999 when she took a $2,000 stock trading account and grew it to over $2 million. Without her input and assistance, I never would have been able to put into words what has been a blessing for so many. Or Jerry Guite, who was the source of so many introductions to successful entrepreneurs and investors throughout my life and a key encourager for me to create my own path. There are many others who provided input and inspiration including David McShane, Erik Dodds, Michael Kramer, Aaron Adams, Clint Coons, Patti Peery, Michael Bowman and David Gass, just to name a few; but the point is that this is not a work of one man's opinion. This is a path paved by the experiences of many that I simply point out so that you can follow their example and get similar results.

ENDNOTES

---

1 Anne Tergesen and Gretchen Morgenson, "Unions' Tactic Hurts Teachers' Nest Egg," *The Wall Street Journal,* December 19, 2019.

2 United States Government Accountability Office, "Retirement Security: Most Households Approaching Retirement Have Low Savings," GAO 15-419 (May 2015).

3 Kenneth Kim, "How Much Do Mutual Funds Really Cost?" *Forbes,* September 24, 2016, https://www.forbes.com/sites/kennethkim/2016/09/24/how-much-do-mutual-funds-really-cost/#1899a724a527.

4 Personal Capital, "Hidden Beneath the Surface: What Americans Are Paying in Advisory Fees," undated, accessed December 6, 2019, https://www.personalcapital.com/assets/public/Personal-Capital-Advisor-Fee-Report.pdf/.

5 Board of Governors of the Federal Reserve, "Consumer Credit—G.19," August 7, 2020, https://www.federalreserve.gov/releases/g19/HIST/cc_hist_tc_levels.html.

6 Yuka Hayashi, "Credit-Card Debt in the U.S. Rises to Record $930 Billion," *The Wall Street Journal,* February 12, 2020.

7 IRS, "SOI Tax Stats-IRS Data Book," June 30, 2020, https://www.irs.gov/statistics/soi-tax-stats-irs-data-book.

8 U.S. Bureau of Labor Statistics, "Consumer Price Index for All Urban Consumers: Owners' Equivalent Rent of Residences in U.S. City Average," August 12, 2020, https://fred.stlouisfed.org/series/CUSR0000SEHC.

9 Alina Comoreanu, "Credit Card Landscape Report," WalletHub. August 13, 2020, https://wallethub.com/edu/cc/credit-card-landscape-report/24927/.

10 Roge Karma, "The Gross Inequality of Death in America," *The New Republic,* May 10, 2019, https://newrepublic.com/article/153870/inequality-death-america-life-expectancy-gap.

11 Data based on free quotes obtained from Yahoo! Finance.